Differentiated Assessment for Middle and High School Classrooms

Deborah Blaz

Routledge
Taylor & Francis Group
New York London

First Published 2008 by Eye On Education

Published 2013 by Routledge
711 Third Avenue, New York, NY, 10017, USA
2 Park Square, Milton Park, Abingdon, Oxon OX14 4RN

Routledge is an imprint of the Taylor & Francis Group, an informa business

Copyright © 2008, Taylor & Francis.

Library of Congress Cataloging-in-Publication Data

Blaz, Deborah.
   Differentiated assessment for middle and high school classrooms / by Deborah Blaz.
      p.cm.
   Includes bibliographical references.
   ISBN 978-1-59667-077-8
1. Educational evaluation. 2. Learning--Evaluation. I. Title.
   LB2822.75.B53 2008
   373.126'4--dc22

                                                            2007050700
ISBN: 978-1-59667-077-8 (pbk)

Also Available from EYE ON EDUCATION

**Teacher-Made Assessments: Connecting
Curriculum, Instruction, and Student Learning**
Christopher R. Gareis and Leslie W. Grant

**Short-Cycle Assessment: Improving Student
Achievement Through Formative Assessment**
Lang, Stanley, and Moore

**Formative Assessment for English Language Arts:
A Guide for Middle and High School Teachers**
Amy Benjamin

**Performance-based Learning and Assessment
in Middle School Science**
K. Michael Hibbard

**Assessment in Middle and High School
Mathematics: A Teacher's Guide**
Daniel Brahier

What Every Teacher Needs to Know about Assessment
Leslie Wilson

**Teaching, Learning, and Assessment Together:
The Reflective Classroom**
Arthur Ellis

**A Collection of Performance Tasks and Rubrics:
Primary School Mathematics**
Charlotte Danielson and Pia Hansen Powell

Upper Elementary School Mathematics
Charlotte Danielson

Middle School Mathematics
Charlotte Danielson

High School Mathematics
Charlotte Danielson and Elizabeth Marquez

**What Great Teachers Do *Differently*:
14 Things That Matter Most**
Todd Whitaker

About the Author

Deborah Blaz, a French teacher at Angola High School in Angola, Indiana, is a native of St. Charles, Illinois. She received her B.A. in French and German from Illinois State University; a diploma from the Université de Grenoble in Grenoble, France; and, in 1974, an M.A. in French from the University of Kentucky. She also completed requirements for a minor in English from Indiana University in 1979. Ms. Blaz has taught French and English to grades 7 through 12 for the past 28 years in Indiana. She also serves as foreign language department chair at her school, does professional translation work, and volunteers as an English instructor at the local literacy coalition.

Ms. Blaz is the author of five best-selling reference books: *The Foreign Language Teacher's Guide to Active Learning*; *Teaching Foreign Languages in the Block*; *A Collection of Performance Tasks and Rubrics: Foreign Languages*; *Bringing the Standards for Foreign Language Learning to Life*; and *Differentiated Instruction: A Guide for Foreign Language Teachers*. A member of many professional associations, she has frequently presented on successful teaching strategies at state, regional, and national conferences; many universities; and high schools. She is also a keynote speaker. In addition to receiving the Project E Excellence in Education award in 2000, she was also named Indiana's French Teacher of the Year by the Indiana chapter of the American Association of Teachers of French (IAATF) in 1996 as well as to the All-USA Teacher Team, Honorable Mention, by *USA Today* in 1996. She may be contacted at Angola High School, 350 S. John McBride Avenue, Angola, IN 46703 or by e-mail: dblaz@msdsc.org

Acknowledgements

Thanks to the following contributors: Nina Kendall, social studies teacher at Eagle's Landing High School in McDonough, Georgia; Marcia Losco, social studies teacher at Yorktown Middle School in Yorktown, Indiana; and Shelly Barnes, physical education teacher at Scotland High School in Laurinburg, North Carolina.

TABLE OF CONTENTS

1

Why Differentiate?

How diverse is your classroom in terms of the following characteristics?

♦ Cognitive abilities

♦ Confidence in learning

♦ Cultural/ethnic influences

♦ Gender influences

♦ How students value learning

♦ Interest in the subject you teach

♦ Learning pace

♦ Learning styles (visual, spatial, auditory, tactile, kinesthetic, etc.)

♦ Readiness

♦ Socioeconomic and family characteristics

Without question, every teacher will, after examining this list, think of many different aspects of diversity present in every classroom. Considering all these different influences, the question is not really, "Why differentiate?" but "How?"

The purpose of this book is not to teach you how to create or structure a differentiated lesson or unit; it is to teach you how to evaluate students before, during, and after a unit is taught, and how to use differentiation when performing this evaluation. It is designed to complement general books on differentiation, which generally concentrate on differentiating the content (presentation) or process (practice) portions of a lesson, and act as a resource for people who have been introduced to differentiation but want to know more about how to integrate assessment into the process.

First, let's briefly review what assessment is. In an educational context, assessment is a process, not a one-time event. It is a series of episodes in the learning process, part reflection, part understanding of and documenting progress in achievement of learning objectives. Behavior is adjusted based on assessment results.

There are four basic steps to assessment:

The *purpose* portion usually requires a determination of what students need to know, how to find out if they have learned it, and how to motivate students to want to achieve the desired result. The *information* portion involves observing, describing, collecting, recording, and scoring knowledge, skills, attitudes and beliefs. *Interpretation*, even more importantly, calls for examining the results of the assessment and using it to *reflect* how to improve both instruction and learning. Frankly, these last two steps are not really assessment (basically collecting data) but are in fact *evaluation steps, in which the assessment data is compared to standards to judge their worth or quality, and to adjust instruction accordingly.*

In my experience outside higher academic/scientific circles, however, the word *assessment* is generally used (albeit erroneously) to include both assessment and evaluation. Therefore, in this book those concepts are intertwined and simply referred to as *assessment*.

Assessment is an important component in any classroom, differentiated or not; and it is my hope that this book helps its readers to better comprehend the potential, as well as the importance of a good assessment, and use a wider variety of assessment to better address the needs of students.

As always assessment should follow several guidelines:

- *Assess daily.*

- *Be formative whenever possible:* a *temperature check* not just to measure knowledge but to give feedback.

- *Ask students to apply the knowledge and skills* gained in basically the same way they have practiced that knowledge and skills. There should be a clear match between the expected outcomes of a unit and the tasks provided as the assessment.

- *Be timely,* make results quickly available to the student.

- *Extend knowledge, rather than merely measure it.*

- *Never surprise students.* Tell them what they'll learn, how to learn it, and how they'll know they've learned it. No pop quizzes, no surprise categories. Test what was taught following the same manner in which it was practiced.

- *Have clear criteria* (a checklist and/or rubric) that communicate how students will be assessed.

♦ *Be authentic*. Students should be asked to perform in as close to a real-life situation as possible in a classroom.

If you wish to improve student performance and not just measure it, students should do the following:

♦ Know right from the start what they are expected to learn.

♦ Study models of high performance and monitor their own progress, much like professional athletes or actors.

♦ Ask each other or the teacher, "How can I improve this?" or "How can I find more evidence to support my conclusion?"

♦ Achieve at their highest possible level.

♦ Have opportunities to learn from the assessment, and show this learning in future assessments.

Why Differentiate?

Once again, in assessing students, we can't assume that *one size fits all*. The method of evaluation used should be a continuation of the type of differentiation used in the unit. In other words, assessment should be linked to the following:

♦ Method of performance during practice of a skill or concept

♦ Student learning styles

♦ Level of cognitive ability (Bloom's or another)

♦ Student skill level

Dr. Carol Ann Tomlinson (1995), national expert on and proponent of differentiation, succinctly defines differentiation:

Differentiation allows students multiple options for taking in information, making sense of ideas, and expressing what they have learned. A differentiated classroom provides different avenues to acquiring content, to processing or making sense of ideas, and to developing products so that each student can learn effectively.

What Is Differentiated Assessment?

I'd like to comment on two aspects of Tomlinson's model of a differentiated classroom that particularly apply to the assessment portion of instruction:

1. Students are *active* in setting goals based on student readiness, interests, and abilities. They may choose the topic and plan the practice, but they should also help decide how and when they want to be

evaluated, as well as whether they should be evaluated on the basis of growth or of attainment. This gives them a feeling of ownership in their own learning process and of partnership with the instructor, and generally motivates as well as empowers them. Motivation is an important factor in learning and is all too often underemphasized in the assessment phase.

2. Assessment of student readiness and growth is *ongoing* and built into the curriculum. Teachers continuously assess student readiness and interest to provide support when students need additional instruction and guidance as well as evaluate when a student or group of students is ready to move ahead to another phase of curriculum.

Grading in a Differentiated Classroom

In a differentiated classroom there should also be separate grades given for three aspects:

1. Growth (changes in performance/knowledge/skills from beginning to end of the unit)

2. Achievement (actual standards-based performance)

3. Effort

Grades should *not* be based on the following:

♦ Preassessments

♦ Timeliness of performance

Other than those basic concepts, there's actually nothing special or new about using assessment in a differentiated situation.

Types of Assessments Used

There are three types of assessment used in differentiation:

1. *Preassessments* determine readiness and make decisions on how to differentiate (see Chapter 2 for more information).

2. *Formative assessments* provide feedback for both student and teacher on how learning is progressing during instruction (Chapter 3 deals specifically with this sort of assessment). It is also an opportunity to facilitate intervention (identify students having difficulties) and provide enrichment (for students who have clearly mastered content).

3. *Summative (or formal) assessments* are done at the end of a concept, process, or unit to evaluate student mastery and teacher effectiveness. They reflect the standards and objectives of instruction and should show students' mastery levels on all essential and enduring knowledge for the concepts being studied. The results should be used to evaluate student achievement (what do they still need more practice on?) *and* teacher performance (by the teacher: How effective were my strategies/techniques? How could I do this better next time?) and adjust instruction based on the results of the assessment data. Examples of summative assessments would include science lab reports, journal entries, performance tasks, portfolios, unit tests, semester exams, products, exhibits, or demonstrations. Chapters 4 through 6 as well as Appendix 1 on "Ways to Show What You Know" contain many examples.

Many teachers use a lot of energy on the final assessment, but these have limited effect on learning. Students generally can't use the feedback from these as well, because in many cases when the unit is over, they begin to master new skills or very different topics. Teachers can still use the results to guide them next time they teach that unit, however, and might be able to *spiral* some repractice of needed material during the next unit.

A Few More Observations About Differentiating Assessment

♦ An assessment is not just a test at the end of a unit. It is ongoing. Its purpose is either to screen and identify those who need assistance or help plan instruction as well as provide feedback for both the teacher and the student.

♦ In designing instruction, teachers need assessment that reflects student learning, achievement, motivation, and attitudes on instructionally relevant classroom activities. One of the best ways to think about pursuing such assessment is to view it as an *interactive* process.

♦ Students need multiple ways to demonstrate their learning: tests (individual as well as partner and group tests) as well as observations, interviews, self-evaluations, and many other formats to be found in more detail later in this book.

♦ Assessments identify both what is right and what is wrong, and suggest how to fix what is wrong.

Important Elements in Designing a Differentiated Assessment

Now let's get away from the general and look at three specific aspects of an assessment.

Perhaps the most important factor in a successful assessment is the presence of scaffolding.

Scaffolding

When I first heard the word *scaffolding* I thought it referred to the structure of a building. It does refer to structure and is used in many aspects of education to guide students. Feedback and assessment are two forms of scaffolding.

Scaffolding in assessment has several aspects:

◆ It provides clear directions.

◆ It clarifies *why we are doing this* (motivation and purpose).

◆ It keeps students on task. They always know what to do next.

◆ It also keeps students from *straying from the path* of the assignment, focusing them on what information they need to find and use as well as suggesting resources free of bias, the correct reading level, and of good quality.

◆ It helps students more efficiently use their time because there's no waiting for others or for someone to come check their work; they can do it themselves.

◆ It clarifies expectations by referring to rubrics that define and illustrate excellence. When the criteria are clear, students know what quality work is.

◆ It can be used by students and teachers to determine successful completion of the task: There are no surprises or disappointments and no uncertainty, because it is clear to all who use it if the job has been completed and, if so, how satisfactorily.

At the onset of an activity, scaffolding takes the form of narrowing down the topic and incorporating some creativity. For example, if you tell a student, "Find out all you can about France" you may get pages and pages of barely digested (and possibly plagiarized) text; but if you ask, "Would you like to move to France?" you have changed it from a simple finding-and-gathering exercise to one that requires shopping for information, cooking and digesting it to produce answers.

For such an assignment, then, the scaffolding might look like this:

WHO	Name:
WHAT	Decide if you would like to live in France
WHY	List some reasons why people might move to another country: 1. 2. 3. 4. Now put a star (*) next to ones that might influence you to move.
WHERE	Now, go to France and pick a city: _____, using ONLY these web sites/resources (teacher should select sites or media resources that are of good quality, unbiased, and at the correct reading level): Now tell something about each of these for that city: Important sites: Geographical features (rivers, mountains, etc.) Population: Products known for: Transportation: Education: Cultural events:
WHICH	Put your decision here, followed by at least three reasons for your decision:

The best scaffolding uses at least one of these question words: why, how, or which.

- *Why* requires analysis of cause and effect as well as the listing of variables in a situation. It leads naturally to a *how* or *which* conclusion. Constructivist learning always asks why.

- *How* is a good problem-solving and synthesis question.

- *Which* asks students to decide between alternatives, to make up their minds.

None of these three involve mere recall, but focus instead on higher Bloom's processes. Here are three more general examples:

Assessment	Without Scaffolding	With Scaffolding
Write a word problem.	Create a word problem.	After reading an example, fill out the outline of a word problem. Include an equation, story, and question as well as the answer.
Summarize a science experiment.	Write a lab report.	Given a list of procedures in science experiments, and questions to answer, follow it using actual materials. Then write down the steps you followed and your observations during this process, summarizing your results and stating your conclusions. Make sure you answered all the questions and evaluate the results (why did you get these results?). Suggest follow-up activities or variations on the experiment.
Retell or summarize a text.	Write five main ideas from an article and give examples.	Complete an outline, a list, or a semantic map. How was the article organized? Make at least one suggestion to improve it.

Here are some currently available (January2008) online examples of units with significant amounts of scaffolding:

♦ The Active Science classroom, provides scaffolding for creating science units for students: http://www.bcps.org/offices/lis/staging/activesci/index.htm

♦ Interactive Research guide, PowerPoint on how to do good research: http://www.bcps.org/offices/lis/curric/

♦ The WebQuest Page, with instructions on how to create WebQuest emphasizing scaffolding: http://webquest.sdsu.edu/

Graphic Organizers

I also love using graphic organizers as scaffolding: When they are completely filled out, students know they have found the necessary information, and enough of it, to go on to another step, take the test, or do whatever is next in their differentiated unit. At present and for free, http://www.teachnology.com/worksheets/graphic/ has 44 different types of worksheets using graphics to help students study just about anything I can think of.

For example, in a literature unit, you could have students fill in a time line or flow chart with the events in the plot; a Venn diagram to compare and contrast two locales, characters, or poems; a brainstorming web during a discussion; or a spider web to show relationships between characters. I still remember doing one for *War and Peace* to keep track of characters and all their nicknames, as well as bloodlines and friendships.

Product Descriptors

A product descriptor is a sort of checklist or bulleted list of requirements to which students may refer to know what information to include and steps to take.

Students have lots of questions when beginning an assignment. These may include the following:

♦ How long must this be? How many words or pages are required?

♦ How many sources must be cited? What types of resources are needed?

♦ Should my argument be logical? How should it be organized?

♦ Does spelling count?

♦ Does originality count?

♦ Should there be a title? Footnotes? A bibliography?

♦ Are there special terms or strategies I need to use?

Here is a sample product descriptor for a science lab report:

Section	Points	What's Needed
Format		♦ Name of each section at left side of paper ♦ All words spelled correctly ♦ Either typed or very neatly written ♦ Paper in good condition (no dirt or rips)
Title		♦ Centered at the top of the page ♦ States purpose of lab (describes the lab done) ♦ Date performed ♦ Due date ♦ Performed by teacher ♦ Performed by course

Section	Points	What's Needed
Question		♦ Single sentence that states the question that the investigation seeks to answer
Hypothesis		♦ A single sentence that predicts the outcome of the investigation
Materials		♦ List of all materials and, where appropriate, the exact amounts used
Method		♦ Written in the past tense (i.e., "The beaker was filled with a mild acid solution.") ♦ Explains step by step what was done in the experiment; each step numbered ♦ Clear and detailed enough for a reader to perform the same experiment
Results		♦ Record of data collected in investigation (data table, graphs, observations, calculations used) ♦ Objectively reported (no explanation of results)
Conclusion		♦ One sentence stating whether the results support your hypothesis, followed by two or three more sentences providing reasons why the experiment does or does not support it ♦ One paragraph explaining the following: • Where error might have occurred in experiment • How that error could be reduced in future experiments

Rubrics

A rubric is a list of explicit criteria for assessing student performance or product. In differentiation, a rubric is an essential component. Unlike product descriptors, which are most often provided by teachers, students often help write the rubrics that are used to evaluate them (this is a good formative assessment because it asks them to examine what they have learned so far and make judgments about it).

How I've changed my opinion of what a rubric should look like:

♦ Most online rubric-making software (and even my previous book on writing rubrics) begins with a description of the lowest possible performance. I think this should be reversed, with the best performance criteria first, especially because students who don't read well start at the left and possibly not read all the way over.

♦ There should be a fifth column with a challenging option, when possible: something to involve the gifted students, to suggest options for performances above-and-beyond the level required.

There are basically two types of rubric: holistic and analytic.

Holistic Rubric

A holistic rubric evaluates the performance overall and rates it in a qualitative manner. Here is an example of a holistic rubric for a science handout:

	Outstanding	On Track	Emerging	Off Track	WOW
Content	All relevant information is presented and accurate	Some details are missing, only describes briefly	Some errors, no history given	Major errors, names few of the principles, topic not explained	Eye-catching method of organization
Diagram	Fully labeled and clearly illustrates principles	Not fully labeled but illustrates principles	Messy, few labels, principles unclear	No diagram	Well-chosen pictures in addition to diagram
Neatness	Easy to read, spelling/grammar correct	Few spelling/grammar errors, easy to read	Several spelling/grammar errors	Messy, many spelling/grammar errors	
Overall impression	Descriptive title, page full of information, easy to understand	Appropriate title, fairly well explained, and meets minimum length of 1 page	Title unrelated to information, some sections hard to follow	No title, too short/too long, material is plagiarized/copied	Creative and colorful cover, creates lots of interest

Now let's compare the two types of rubrics when used to assess something like behavior or growth, rather than a specific assignment. Here is an example of a holistic rubric for student and teachers to use to assess behavior:

Daily Performance Grade

9–10 Exceeds the standard	Helps facilitate classroom activity all the time. Demonstrates engaged active learning throughout the period. Makes consistently strong contributions to the classroom.
8 Meets the standard	Participates in a generally constructive way. Demonstrates engaged active learning through part of the class period. Makes some strong contributions to the classroom.
7 Approaches the standard	Has little negative or positive effect on the class. May tackle concepts but shows little evidence of learning. Prepares but makes little contribution to the classroom.
1–6 Falls below the standard	Has more of a negative effect on the class than positive. Required work or preparation incomplete. Disruptive behavior makes learning difficult for others. Has trouble staying on task; needs to be reminded.
0 Fails to meet standard	Sent out of class or truant. Refuses to stay on task. Sleeps.
Extra points as determined by teacher: **Wow**	Suggests effective improvements in instruction, methods of practice, motivational strategies or behavior management. May even help create materials for instructional use.

Analytical Rubric

An analytical rubric breaks the performance down into the different levels of behavior expected, assigning each a point value (which can be weighted if desired), which are totaled for a quantitative measure. Here is an example of an analytical rubric for growth in an English class (and which, in my opinion, needs a *wow* category):

	4 **Exceeds Standard**	3 **Meets Standard**	2 **Standard Barely Met**	1 **Unacceptable**
Work/Effort	Work done well (more than minimum effort); shows leadership.	Work mostly correct; works well on own or in group.	Grammatically incorrect, simple sentences, misspellings common; work done on time.	Work not done or late; plagiarism/copying; sleeping, tardiness, or excessive absence.
Skill	Succeeds in using new vocabulary.	Consistently attempts to use new vocabulary or structures.	Little attempt to use new vocabulary or structures.	No attempt to use new vocabulary or structures.
Behavior/ Attitude	Encourages and helps others. Exceeds expectations.	Enthusiastic and cooperative.	Obeys all rules with occasional reminder needed.	Comments are incomprehensible, inappropriate or disruptive.

Here is a rubric for a weekly composition whose purpose is to improve overall writing skills, to practice current vocabulary and grammar.

	4	3	2	1
Content	Responds to all parts of prompt; creative and interesting	General comments only	Addresses part of prompt	Does not address prompt
Vocabulary	Uses many words from recent study	Uses several new vocabulary words	Several poor word choices, awkward phrasing	Only uses basic vocabulary
Grammar	Perfect or nearly perfect	Some errors in focus grammar usage	Many errors in focus grammar usage	Little attempt to use focus grammar

Organization	Logical and thoughtful	Mostly logical	Attempt at organization is apparent	Difficult or impossible to follow
Mechanics and Spelling	Perfect or nearly perfect	One or two major errors	Several important errors	Failure to proofread
Total: _____ / 20 points				

The following resources were all free and available online in August 2007:

- A great resource for writing analytical rubrics of many types: http:// www.teach-nology.com/web_tools/rubrics/

- A collection of ready-to-print rubrics that both student and teacher can use, and which can become a digital checklist in an HTML editor: http://www.bcpl.net/~sullivan/modules/tips/assess_sec.html

- A useful tool for writing math and science rubrics: http://www.exemplars.com/online_assessment/index.html

Checklists

Another type of rubric, a checklist is exactly what it sounds like. It is a list of behaviors to look for; the presence or absence of each attribute is recorded by checking or circling that action. Checklists are often incorporated in product descriptors, as well as used for assessment purposes, especially in *performance* situations in classes such as music, family and consumer sciences, or physical education classes. Lots of free, useable checklists, in both English and Spanish, are found online at http://pblchecklist.4teachers.org/.

Important ideas to keep in mind when using rubrics:

- Be wary of rubrics with odd-numbered levels (as in the popular 5 levels often provided by textbook companies). Not only is there a clear center (3)—and research shows people often choose this rather than decide whether something falls on the better or worse side—but also the five often are interpreted as standard A, B, C, D, and F letter grades; such assumptions may cause resentment or misunderstandings.

- Always give (or have students write) rubrics at the beginning of an exercise or activity so there are no surprises, and students stay focused during the preparation period of the activity. Then you can add the *wow* portion.

♦ In writing rubrics, teachers should evaluate the rubric using Bloom's taxonomy to make sure the *outstanding* and *wow* parts are using higher-level thinking strategies. Also, more weight should be given to parts of the rubric in which students use creative tactics than to those that deal with neatness or following directions. Although giving points for basic, lower-level behaviors is an easy way to build in points that any student can achieve, too much emphasis on these in terms of points toward a grade stifles the urge to be creative or produce something amazing.

♦ You might consider having students use the rubric, and having a peer use it (or the whole class) instead of just the teacher. I recommend doing this.

On the next page is a good 4-point rubric for a speech for a total of 100 points:

Speaker:				
Speech title:				
	Strong (4) creative, interesting	**Detailed (3)** consistent presence	**Basic (2)** some evidence	**Weak (1)** little or no evidence
Content:				
♦ Purpose				
♦ Details				×2
♦ Topic				
Organization				
♦ Introduction				
♦ Body				×2
♦ Conclusion				×2
Language				
♦ Appropriate vocabulary				
♦ Deliberate word usage and style				
Voice				
♦ Tone & control				
♦ Speed & tempo				
♦ Emphasis				
♦ Proper pronunciation				
♦ Volume				
Physical behavior				
♦ Posture				×2
♦ Gestures				×2
♦ Facial expression				
Communication				
♦ Projection				
♦ Responsiveness				

And here is one more for a science presentation, which also takes into account the affect/understandability of the performance, an aspect often overlooked in rubrics:

	Genius	Smart	Average	Redo
Content	Relevant, clear, complete and accurate info	Some missing details; too brief	No history given; incomplete information; some small errors	Major errors in information; few or no principles named or examples given
Presentation	Lots of eye contact, speaks without referring to notes; involves fellow students; speaks clearly at appropriate volume	Some eye contact, little need for notes; varies voice at times; some involvement with fellow students	No eye contact; uses notes frequently; little involvement with fellow students	Reads from notes, no involvement with fellow students; too loud or soft; speaks in a monotone
Visual aids	Aids make words more easily understood; held student interest	Messy in appearance	Poorly organized, adds little to presentation	No visual aids
Understanding of topic	Shows outstanding comprehension of topic and good ability to explain it to others	Shows good understanding of topic	Incomplete understanding of topic; cannot answer questions	Poor understanding of material
Organization	Logical pattern with smooth transitions between sections	Only a few rough spots	Information not given in logical sequence	Appears to move randomly from one idea to the next
Creativity	Keeps everyone interested	Some students appear distracted	Fails to maintain interest	Fails to capture and maintain interest

Student-Negotiated Standards

In this highly effective method of assessment, students set personal standards that they use to guide and evaluate their own progress. This method has been used successfully in industry for quite a while, and many in education have been championing it for years. Here's how I generally do this:

- ♦ I show or distribute some examples of previous work (papers, poems, stories, posters, etc.) done by other students (a different class or from previous years). I ask students to look at them and tell me which are best and why. We make a list of the characteristics they find desirable and that become the descriptor for an A effort. Then they help me write the rubric or checklist:

  - What is not absolutely necessary?

  - What can be partially done?

  - What is good, but not great?

  - What does a really bad product look like?

- ♦ I also teach the students to assess their own work or that of others by using a rubric or checklist. I don't worry if their scores don't agree with mine (many are reluctant to criticize friends or popular students), but we talk about why our scores disagree so that we're *on the same page* about expectations.

Not only do the students remember the standards better, because they suggested them, they are more likely to want to achieve them, because they are trying to please their peers and not just the teacher. Also, they perceive their evaluation as more *fair*.

Fairness in Differentiation

Students respond to the situation that they perceive, and it is not necessarily the same situation that we have defined. It is imperative to be aware of this routine divergence between intention and actuality in ... teaching ... becoming aware of it is part of what it means to teach well. (Flint, 1998, p. 1)

First, let me state that fairness when using differentiation is no different from fairness in any other classroom situation. The strategies and results are the same. As educators, we carefully plan units to fit students' needs and expand their education in a fair manner. But when differentiating, the potential for being perceived as *unfair* increases, because students are often asked to produce different results at differing levels of difficulty and graded using different rubrics; so it is imperative to ensure that students, parents, and administrators recognize that what you are asking students to do is *fair*. Fairness is not just designing a course that correlates closely with standards and curriculum and allows for differing student abilities and interests. What is needed is what I'd call *good practices*.

A perception of unfairness by students can undermine the trust between student and teacher that must exist for effective instruction and learning, so we need to carefully examine policies and behaviors and make sure they are not only fair but are *perceived as fair* by students. If students are unhappy, they enlist parents and administrators in support or action against what you are trying to do in your classroom.

There are three types of fairness (listed in the order of importance to students):

1. Interactional

2. Procedural

3. Outcome

Interactional Fairness

You'd expect students to be most concerned with outcome or procedural, but they're not! When students perceive your behavior toward them as unfair, they stop trying to learn, so attention to this aspect is crucial. According to Rodabaugh (1996) there are five aspects: impartiality, respect, concern, integrity, and propriety.

1. Students expect everyone to be treated equally well. Allowing some students to dominate discussions, calling on some more than others, being friendlier toward some, and similar behaviors, are things to avoid.

2. Respect means politeness, basically. Impatience, demeaning words, not listening to students' ideas, body language, facial expression, or even posture that conveys disrespect are all thought to be inappropriate by students. Civility and calm in a difficult situation, as well as holding private meetings with students who offend by, for example, sleeping in class, are what is regarded as fair.

3. Demonstrating concern is easy: Students want to know their voice is heard in your classroom. Learn students' names, talk to them before and after class, answer questions in a thoughtful manner, and help those having difficulties. This may be tough with really big classes, but here are a few additional tips, from the study by Whitley, Perkins, Balogh, Keith-Spiegel, and Wittig (2000):

- ♦ Help students get to know one another early on, by briefly introducing themselves. Tell the class a bit about yourself and your own background as well.

- ♦ Be available: Make yourself available before and after class to talk with students, and give students your e-mail address or other contact information, or devise another way (comments box or something like that) to encourage comments and questions.

- ♦ Be proactive about inviting students to come to you for help.

- ♦ Use as many collaborative and small-group activities and discussions as possible.

- ♦ Share what you have learned with students when you return from an absence to attend a professional meeting.

- ♦ Have students periodically fill out feedback forms, and respond to those openly in the classroom.

4. Be consistent and truthful. Explain policies, procedures and why they are needed (especially, correlate them to educational goals). Also, make sure to use the rewards or penalties involved in these policies all the time. And when you don't know something, admit it.

5. Respect students' feelings. Listen to them, reply thoughtfully to their questions, prepare them for emotionally upsetting content in a reading or film, don't require them to reveal personal information in class, and maintain appropriate social distance (including jokes or stories), both during class and at school events.

Procedural Fairness

Again, Rodabaugh (1996) describes four aspects, or factors, for perceived fairness in procedures: work load, tests, providing feedback, and student input.

1. Evaluating course content for a good *fit* between the work load and students' aptitude is crucial in differentiating; and if they complain, listen to their input and review your choices, if it seems appropriate. Also consider (somewhat) other factors such as employment and extracurricular activities they may all have. Of course, differentiation of content for students' interests and abilities (and explaining to students how and why you have done this) goes a long way toward making them regard their assessment as fair, because they have contributed toward it.

2. Tests are perceived as fair if all material on the test was covered in class and is relevant to the learning objectives they were given, all

questions are appropriately difficult (no *gotcha*/flunk-out questions), and the questions as well as the response options are clearly stated. Again, there's nothing wrong with letting students contribute questions for a test, or suggest products on which they'd like to be evaluated.

3. Feedback needs to be prompt and helpful, and it should go both ways. Discuss questions that many missed and why the answer was wrong, and carefully consider the validity of any student complaints about a test. Another idea: I always put feedback questions on the final page of my tests: "I can (circle: well/somewhat/not at all) do _____ (learning objective)" or "I still need more help with _____" and similar feedback opportunities.

To summarize: Students who are given a part to play in selecting a topic, designing a project and/or their assessment, and whose feedback and opinions are listened to are more likely to regard the outcome as fair.

Outcome Fairness

Students want to see fair grading practices. In addition to clearly worded questions and instructions on tests (discussed previously), to foster perception of your grading practices as fair, make sure to do the following:

♦ Tell students how they will be graded, from the very beginning of the class (or unit). Provide rubrics or checklists so students can self-evaluate as well. (And don't forget to involve students in designing those rubrics or checklists whenever possible!)

♦ Base students' grades only on his/her individual performance or individual contribution to group work (include peer assessments done by the group, and/or individual papers based on a group assignment).

♦ Use multiple assessments. Not only does this provide more accurate information than just one measure, it affords students a chance to show learning according to both stronger and weaker learning styles.

When to Differentiate

Differentiation is the recognition of and commitment to plan for student differences...The goals of a differentiated classroom are to maximize student growth and to promote individual student success.

—Curry School of Education, University of Virginia

Although standardized tests, unit tests, and quizzes are necessary and helpful for placement purposes and determining grades, they do not provide enough information for teachers to evaluate students' depth of understanding. To really evaluate students, we must observe throughout the year how students solve problems, evaluate students' writing, and listen carefully to the students' discussions and explanations about their thinking. Differentiation allows us to do that.

By using ongoing assessment, the hallmark of differentiation, teachers can accommodate differences by providing students with multiple means for expressing what they know, such as the option to respond by writing, speaking, drawing, creating an animation or video, or developing a multimedia presentation. When students get to use a format with which they are comfortable, they are more likely to be able to (and want to) show what they know and can do.

Differentiation also allows students to make choices, self-evaluate, and produce a product that reflects their potential and that they are proud of. Students in a differentiated classroom learn a lot about the following:

- *Real problems:* When assignments are chosen by students, they can be real and relevant to the student and the activity.

- *Real audiences:* Use an audience that is appropriate for the product, which could include another student or group of students, teacher (not necessarily the class teacher), assembly, mentor, community, or specific interest group.

- *Real deadlines:* Encourage time-management skills and realistic planning.

- *Transformations:* Involve original manipulation of information rather than regurgitation or recall of data.

- *Appropriate evaluation:* The product and the process of its development are both self-evaluated and evaluated by the product's audience using previously established real world criteria that are appropriate for such products.

Summary

The reasons for differentiating *assessment* are as compelling as those for differentiating the content or process portions of a unit. Scaffolding and rubrics are a basic and necessary component of the assessment process. Assessment should be constant (before, during and after the unit), come in a variety of forms, be easy for students and teachers to use in evaluating themselves and others, and should identify both what is being done wrong and what is being done right. These last concepts will be discussed in much more detail and depth in the chapters that follow.

2

Preassessment

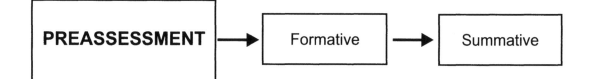

PREASSESSMENT → Formative → Summative

Preassessment is used to determine student readiness (prior knowledge and interests) and make decisions on how to differentiate the idea, concept, process, or unit. Data must be collected for the purpose of guiding instruction. However, because such assessments do *not* reflect student mastery of content, they are *not* to be used to grade students. After doing a preassessment and evaluating the results, the teacher begins instruction for the unit, does formative assessments during the unit itself, and finishes with a summative assessment.

Preassessments include, but are not limited to thew following:

♦ Know, want to know, and learned (KWL) charts (my favorite, defined in Appendix 2)

♦ Pretests

♦ Checklists

♦ Performances while carrying out sample activities

♦ Observations of students

♦ Self-evaluation forms and surveys

♦ Conversations/conferences with individual students

♦ Directed questioning

♦ Results from the previous year's state-mandated tests

♦ Visual organizers like mind maps or webs

♦ Multiple intelligence surveys

♦ Learning style inventories

♦ Interest surveys

♦ Grades from previous years

- Student journals

- Walkabouts, or *roam around the room*

- Student demonstrations

- Administration of the summative assessment, for purposes of compacting (see Chapter 5 for more explanation or Appendix 2 for a brief definition of compacting)

The more varied your group of students are, the more preassessment is needed.

Because at the secondary level it is likely students have prior knowledge of almost any topic to be taught, it is important to preassess to determine what they know, as well as whether they have any misconceptions or false beliefs that may get in the way of instruction (Dochy, Segers, & Buehl, 1999).

Here are some good online examples of preassessment in various subject areas:

- To determine students' knowledge of the Iroquois Confederacy and its influence on our Constitution: http://www.iroquoisdemocracy.pdx.edu/html/assessment.htm

- To see what students know about tides: http://oceandrilling.coe .tamu.edu/curriculum/Sea_Level/Tides/protected/preassess .html

- To preassess students' knowledge of microgravity for a physics class: http://www.texarkanacollege.edu/physci/Nova/ phPreAssess.htm

A lesson with preassessment for food science class: http://www.uen.org/ Lessonplan/preview.cgi?LPid=1185

Use of Preassessment Strategies

In Miner and Finn's (2003) online article on the use of preassessment, the following preassessment strategies were reported by 202 teachers as being commonly used (in bold print), followed by methods used much less often:

Math Teachers	Language Arts Teachers	Science Teachers	Social Studies Teachers
◆ **Observation of student responses and discussion**	◆ **Observation of student responses and discussion**	◆ **Observation of student responses and discussion**	◆ **Observation of student responses and discussion**
◆ **Example activities**	◆ **Observation of student performance on project or product**	◆ **Observation of student performance on project or product**	◆ Example activities
◆ Observation of student performance on project or product	◆ **Journal writing**	◆ Example activities	◆ Observation of student performance on project or product
◆ Journal writing	◆ Example activities	◆ Journal writing	◆ Journal writing
◆ Individual conferences	◆ Portfolios	◆ Portfolios	◆ Individual conferences
◆ Pretest	◆ Individual conferences	◆ Individual conferences	◆ Pretest
◆ Portfolios	◆ Results from last year's test	◆ Results from last year's test	◆ Results from last year's test
◆ Results from last year's test	◆ Student grades from previous yearPretest	◆ Pretest	◆ Portfolios
◆ Student grades from previous year		◆ Student grades from previous year	◆ Student grades from previous year

What was interesting to me was that language arts and math teachers reported more daily use of preassessment than social studies and science teachers. I think this may be because of the skill-building and sequential nature of the subject matter, which would make any variation in prior knowledge and/or ability levels more rapidly obvious.

Also, the method most chosen by all teachers surveyed, you may have noticed, was not on the list I supplied at the beginning of this chapter. I feel strongly that leading a student discussion is not a particularly good method of ascertaining student readiness for those who might comprehend but did not like to participate, and that there might not be sufficient time to include all students in such a discussion. Thus some might not be evaluated at all. Miner and Finn (2003), who also disapproved of this, suggested that this method was chosen because it required little preparation or extra effort on the part of teachers because it was an element usually found in any classroom, differentiated or not. I believe that a good preassessment is well worth the time spent to prepare and administer it.

How to Construct a Preassessment

So, how does one construct a good preassessment? Take a good look at the unit and unpack it using this organizer or any similar one you like.

Standard(s): _____ **Declarative Knowledge** Why do students need to know this?	**Procedural Knowledge (Skills)** What processes do students need to learn? *What should students be able to do years from now?*
What details must students learn? (Keep these to a minimum!)	What skills do students need to learn?
What necessary vocabulary terms or phrases are needed?	What steps and/or rules will students need to follow?

Then, using a format chosen from the list at the beginning of the chapter, or one of your own devising, find out if students know the key terms, steps or rules for that unit. Generally, if 80% mastery is shown, consider compacting or a learning contract for the student. If you don't want to give students a pencil-and-paper preassessment, as for the performing arts, manual arts, physical education or other skills-oriented subjects, consider using a form such as the one following.

Preassessment Template for
Evaluating Student Performance

Unit:	
Indicator	(put curriculum reference/standard here)
Preassessment	(list task students will be asked to do)
Scoring tool	Student performance will be rated: 2: An accurate and thorough response 1: A partial or vague/general response 0: Other
Sample response	(list evaluation cues: key words that should be used, techniques to be observed)
Instructional resources or equipment needed	

3

Formative Assessments and Giving Choices

Preassessment	→	**FORMATIVE**	→	Summative

Let's begin this chapter by agreeing on several things: first, that teaching and learning must be interactive. In the process of that interaction, students perform certain activities.

Teachers will:

1. Assign and/or facilitate activities
2. **Assess student progress and difficulties**
3. Adapt instruction to meet student needs

Students will:

1. Perform chosen activities
2. **Assess own progress**
3. Adapt behavior to learn better

As you can see, formative assessment is the intermediate step in this process for both students and teacher. If the intent of teaching is to get students to think, the intent of formative assessment is to make students' thinking visible to the teacher. Formative assessment should help determine what the students have mastered, what they still need, and what needs to happen next. *Assessment may only be called* formative *when the evidence gathered is actually used to adapt instruction to meet student needs.*

Formative assessment

♦ is daily, if possible, and if not, is very frequently and regularly implemented.

♦ is ongoing.

- is timely: close in time to instruction (e.g., a know, want to know, and learned [KWL]).

- gives helpful feedback and/or advice: honest and specific.

- is done while there's still time to further explain a concept, reteach it, or enlarge on it.

- is actually used to adapt teaching to meet student needs.

- shows amount of effort and/or change that has occurred (progress in learning).

- makes students aware of steps they still need to take/complete (constructive).

- is formal or informal, standardized, and book-generated or home-made; in other words, comes in a wide variety of formats.

- may be reused/ reappear on a summative assessment.

However,

- because learning is still in process at this point in the unit, these assessments should only make up a small percentage, if any, of a student's grade. Student errors at this point should still be expected and not penalized; they *are* still learning, after all.

- it is also crucial not to use approaches in which students are compared with one another, fostering competition rather than personal improvement and achievement. Assessment feedback should not teach low achievers that they have less ability to learn.

- it is essential that the teacher learn something from the assessment, as well as the student. Too many teachers administer several formative assessments and then continue their planned instruction without considering the results!

Why Use Formative Assessment?

In gathering assessments for this book, I quickly realized that most teachers seem to put most of their energy and focus on the final assessment, because law has made these summative assessments, and the data provided about student achievement, of critical importance to the future of schools. However, these have limited affect on learning. Students are unable to use feedback from them to increase their learning or to continue study on that topic. To positively affect learning, energy is better spent on preparing formative assessments, administering and grading/correcting them, and using the information obtained to adjust instruction as needed. These frequent *checkups* are when students learn the most:

♦ Teacher prepares and administers a formative assessment.

♦ Students and teacher get feedback on progress and needs.

♦ Teacher and students adapt instruction to suit current needs.

What is needed then is to break down the *big* test into its component skills, and develop formative assessments of each, so that students, parents, teacher, and administrator can see and evaluate their progress toward mastery of the required skills.

The power of formative assessment may be seen in the well-known effective instructional strategies led by Marzano, Pickering, and Pollock (2001), which identifies providing feedback—a central principle of formative assessment—as one of nine categories of instructional strategies that have statistically significant effects on student achievement.

Common Types of Formative Assessment

Conference (F)	Peer evaluation (F)
Conversation (I)	Performance task (F)
Exit card or exit interview (ticket out) (F)	Physical movement (I)
Journal entry or other reflective tool (I)	Portfolio check (F)
KWL sheet (I)	Questioning session (I)
Notebook check (F)	Quiz (F)
Observation (I)	Self-evaluation (I)

F = formal; I = informal.

♦ *Conferences*

- are dynamic and interactive.

- require questions that focus on student work and ideas.

- help the teacher to understand a student's point of view.

- can be brief and informal or structured and formal.

- usually have a time limit.

Good questions to begin a conference, conversation or interview are as follows:

- I think you were working on (x). How far have you gotten?

- Where did you get this idea?

- What have you been trying to include in your work?

- Tell me about what you are working on today.

- Tell me what sort of help you might need to finish this part.

♦ *Ticket out:* To get out of class at the end of the period, students must write or say something, usually related to the main point of the day's lesson and/or something that they'll be required to know at the end of the unit (or for whatever high-stakes test they give in your state).

♦ *Journal entries* are usually just conversations in written form. Just as in a conversation or conference, students would respond to a question prompt supplied by the teacher.

♦ *Notebook/portfolio check:* This can take various forms, from a checklist such as this self-assessment:

Notebook Check: Assessment Checklist: 10 Points

Student's Name:_____   Score: _____/10

1 point for every item checked below

1. ___ My notebook has an up-to-date table of contents.

2. ___ My notes are in the right order or sequence for this unit of study.

3. ___ I have dated, named, and numbered each page.

4. ___ My notes are neat and easy to read.

5. ___ My notebook has no loose pages (it can pass the test of gravity if held upside down).

6. ___ My notes have been updated to include work missed when absent.

7. ___ All handouts have been included in the right order/sequence.

8. ___ All major assignments are included.

9. ___ All tests and quizzes are included.

10. ___ My notebook says that I am organized.

Or it can be a simple open-notebook quiz over materials students should have in the notebook on that date (an easy way to check if their work has been properly completed and corrected). For more on portfolios, see Chapter 5.

♦ *Observations* are perhaps best done using a checklist. This should be shared with students before the observation takes place (remember, no surprises!), so they know what behaviors you will be expecting.

TASK	Always	Often	Sometimes	Seldom
Selected own topic				
Did prewriting strategy				
Follow structure or pattern				
Uses resources in room				
Works independently				
Stays on task				
Asks for peer or teacher feedback				
Revises work				
Writes legibly and neatly				
Expresses ideas, thoughts and feelings effectively				

♦ *Peer evaluation:* when students evaluate other members of the class, sometimes done anonymously or in a written or oral one-on-one format, and other times in a group or whole-class situation.

The figure on the next page is a sample peer evaluation of a partner's effort during a group project.

Peer Evaluation Sheet

Name of person evaluated: _____

Please use check marks to evaluate your partner's contributions, from 4 (high) to 1 (low).

	4	3	2	1
Demonstrates a positive attitude				
♦ Moves quickly to join group				
♦ Is organized in finding information				
♦ Completes fair share of workload				
♦ Does task agreed upon by group				
Works well with group				
♦ Makes helpful suggestions				
♦ Is a good listener				
♦ Encourages and praises others				
Works well independently				
♦ Meets deadlines				
♦ Shares resources				
♦ Puts information into own words (no plagiarism)				

Total: ___ of 40 points possible

♦ *Physical movement:* This can be the use of manipulatives, such as the well-known cup system, using sets of green, yellow, and red plastic cups. Students working have them on their work surface and if they are working well, the green cup is on top. If they have a question but can continue, the yellow cup is moved to the top position. If they need help and are stuck, the red cup is on top. It is easy to scan a room and see who needs help, instead of interrupting their concentration by asking them how they are doing.

Another movement might be to give a signal, such as a thumbs-up/thumbs-down, or my favorite, *fist-to-five,* in which they show me with their hands how good they feel about their comprehension, one finger meaning not good and five meaning very good. And let's not forget all the classrooms where physical performances are the main focus, such as wood shop, cooking, art, physical education, and so forth. Students demonstrating the correct grip on a piece of equipment before proceeding to the next step, or showing how far they have gotten in an origami piece is a formative assessment.

♦ Self-evaluation: Self-assessment skills are one of the key components of formative assessment. Students should learn to evaluate their own participation, progress, and products, in written or oral form, asking themselves questions:

- What did I learn today?

- Am I done yet?

- What am I doing well?

- What do I need to improve?/What am I having trouble doing?

- Am I making progress?

- What should I do next?

- What surprised me?

- What do I still wonder about?

- In the future, what will I do differently?

Types of Self-Evaluation

Checklist	Interactive notebook
Conference	Interview with teacher
Continuum (i.e., agree-disagree)	Reflection log/journal
Creative performance	Rubric

The end-of-class evaluation I give my level 2 students working on a large group project is shown on the next page.

Student End-of-Project Self-Evaluation

1. What grade would you give yourself for the effort that you put into today's class?

2. What grade would you give your group for its work today?

3. What grade would you give your group for cooperation and effective problem solving today?

4. What percent of what you learned with your group today was new to you?

5. What percent of what you learned from the class today was new to you?

6. Did you learn what you thought you would most like to learn today? If yes, what was it? If you say "no," what will you need to do to learn this?

7. If you could do one thing to make today's class better, what would it be?

The main problem with using self-assessment is that students can only do this well if they have a good, clear picture of the targets they are trying to reach. Many need training to stop viewing themselves as passive subjects and what happens in the classroom as an arbitrary group of activities that are presented to them. There are three essential elements of which students are aware:

1. The desired goal.

2. Where they are right now.

3. How to close the gap between the two preceding elements.

The benefits of using student assessment are that it is open-ended; is student-centered instead of teacher-guided, and encourages students to be responsible for and aware of their own learning and progress and to be reflective about what they are doing. Studies show students who self-evaluate improve their work (Farago, 1994; Beauchamp, McConaghy, Parsons, & Sanford, 1996). They see what they do well as well as where they need to improve. They can set their own goals and even think of ways to improve their learning. Self-evaluation leads to independence on the part of the learner.

Less Common Types of Formative Assessment

As I said earlier, assessments discussed earlier are the more common types of formative assessment. We all tend to teach in the manner we were taught (after all, it worked on us, didn't it?), but part of teaching is recognizing that learning is a lifelong adventure. And, because that means there is always something new to learn, and try, let's investigate some very educationally sound, tested, and useful methods that are a bit more innovative.

Use Choice

Students who are evaluated primarily on one skill that they don't have (or think they don't) are quickly discouraged. I cannot stress enough the importance of using choice in any assessments, as well as in classroom strategies, especially to assure that assessments reflect the choices students have made in their learning strategies. This use of choice results in what is often called a *learning menu* where students make choices, similar to a fixed-price restaurant menu where you might select one each from several appetizers, entrées, side dishes, and desserts. Choosing an entrée would be required, and the dessert part would be for enrichment, extra credit, or early finishers. In any case, the choice is up to the students.

Show-What-You-Know Assessments

This type of assessment is simply when a student is allowed to demonstrate knowledge/mastery of the required skills in a configuration that is chosen by the student.

Skip Questions

This strategy of giving choices can be easy to implement. You can even use parts of a standardized *book* test if desired and build in choice by allowing students to do any three out of five essay questions, or answer six out of ten questions asked of them (writing or saying "pass" or "skip" for the others). I might design a 55-point assessment and allow students to skip any five points (and, because no section has only five points in it, they must still do parts of all of it). I believe this approach mimics real life in any career. If I'm asked to help on a project at school, I can generally choose between leadership and helping roles, or whether I read, write, speak, or just provide refreshments (kinetic activity!). Allowing students to use the chapter skills in the way they are most comfortable with just makes sense to me.

Open-Ended Questions

Open-ended questions are another form of choice, allowing students more leeway in their responses: Pick two famous people off the list provided, and describe their contributions to history; choose three equations and tell what properties you would use to solve them. I like the words *choose* and *tell* because responses could be written or oral, live, or on tape; and I often give my students a choice of those formats.

Write Your Own

A third form of choice involves allowing each student to actually write his or her own assessment. In many chapters, there are a few essential nonnegotiable words or concepts that must be learned. For the rest of the material, have students choose the words or concepts to study, using the following criteria:

- ♦ Select items you've heard but never used or aren't sure how to use.

- ♦ Select topics that seem interesting or useful to you.

Then let students decide both how to practice (see the following for some suggestions) and how it will be assessed. Let students decide what their quiz or test will be: Let each student select what to be evaluated on, and have him or her write the quiz or test (with answer key). Several days later, let each take the quiz over words he or she chose, supplying either the definition or a sentence, depending on your teaching style, their learning level, your choice, or their choice.

They often write more difficult assessments than you might and, in writing them, have to do a lot of Bloom's-style thinking to classify, compare, and evaluate what is important, difficulty levels, and so forth. All of us who have written a test know that this would make them well acquainted with the unit contents.

Send-a-Problem

Send-a-problem is another form of student-designed assessment that is fun to use. It is done in teams of three or four.

+ Decide how many teams of three or four you will have.

+ For each team, prepare a page that is either be numbered or lettered, or a different color of paper so each team's page is unique. If you want to do a permanent version, put a 3-column organizer on poster board and have it laminated; make the left column approximately 2 inches, the right one approximately 3 inches, and the center section the largest.

+ Create as many questions, problems to solve, terms to define, or whatever the desired proficiency is that you wish to evaluate—as many as there are blanks on the page—times the number of teams: Five blanks and five teams = 25 tasks. I save mine on the computer so I can cut down on preparation time the next time I do the unit. Use the curriculum, a review sheet, or look at the summative to see what to include. Print these as strips, and tape a few to each team's sheet so each can be lifted like a flap.

+ Round One: Each group gets a paper, and one colored marker (each team has its own color) and writes the names of the team members on it. On scrap paper, each of them silently does the team's first task. When all are done, they compare answers and decide which one(s) is/are correct and why. Students must correct their answers. Then one of the group lifts the flap and, in the space on the grid, pencils in lightly (must *not* be easily visible) the group's agreed-on answer. This continues for the remaining tasks until all are done, and everyone has his or her corrected paper to keep.

+ Round Two: Have all the groups exchange papers. *Without looking* they follow the same procedure (doing the tasks silently and comparing and correcting), but this time they lift the flap and see what the other team answered. If they like it, they draw something positive in the third column (smiley, rainbow, star, piece of candy, etc.). If not, they draw something negative (frown, road kill, bolt of lightning, or the like; emphasize it should be class appropriate).

♦ Round Three: like round two. I teach on a block schedule, and we have time for all of this in one day; but with shorter periods or if desired, it is possible to do this over two or three days' time, one set each day.

♦ Final Round: Groups gets their original papers back and look at the pictures drawn. If they get a negative drawing, they try to figure out what they did wrong; and if they can't, they send a representative to the other group (they can tell who by the marker color) for help.

This is a good activity because by observing I get feedback on what problems they still have, and because students have to *perform* to please their peers and I get the student-teaching-student dynamic that brain research says results in the best retention of any teaching strategy. It is also good for team building and class morale because of the gamelike structure. (NOTE: Don't forget to have a sponge activity or anchor activity for them, because groups finish at different times.)

Logs

Logs are essentially a journal kept by the student during the learning process, which can be used as evidence of learning.

♦ *Content area logs* are used when students are reading expository texts. Usually in two-column graphic form (or a T-chart) students record *What I Understand* or *What I Don't Understand* (ideas or vocabulary).

♦ *Reading response logs* are generally used when reading literature. In these, students respond to prompts (the generic who/what/where/when/why type, or specific to what is being read) that encourage critical thinking, or they may copy a quote from the text and write a reflection to it.

♦ *Dialog journals* are a form of interactive, ongoing correspondence between two students reading the same selection, or between student and teacher, or, in the case of a summer reading assignment (AP classes often do this) between student and parent or adult reading partner. Students determine the choice of topics, and write questions, answers, or reactions to what the other has written about what they are both reading.

♦ *Narrative logs* are a form of creative writing in which the student retells what is being read from the perspective of a character: Columbus' voyage as told by a sailor on one of his ships, a drop of water in the water cycle, and so forth.

Note that journals can easily be done on audio cassettes, DVDs, or videos as well as in written form.

Grid Assessments

More than one schoolteacher to whom I've spoken gives a tic-tac-toe or bingo-style assessment, either as formative (practice) or as a summative (unit test or final exam). In each box of the grid would be a task students need to perform.

Tic-Tac-Toe

A tic-tac-toe grid has nine boxes. For such a grid, students would be asked to do three tasks horizontally, vertically, or diagonally; but I usually just tell them to do three that *touch*. The key is to have tasks that make them display a variety of skills. They might choose two tasks they really like, but they have to do one that is more of a stretch for them to *connect* the tasks into a group of three.

The teachers I spoke with allow the students to do the tasks in any order they wish; and when the task is performed satisfactorily, they stamp, initial, or mark in some difficult-to-counterfeit manner that space on the grid. For example, if students perform at a satisfactory level, they get a stamp; but if they do not, they may try a second time before it is marked as no longer valid. (This is done to discourage students from trying the task without proper preparation and study, which I found they did when they knew they'd get a second chance if they messed up the first time.)

Here is a sample tic-tac-toe grid for a book report for English that I have used:

Main Character:	Plot:	All Characters:
Draw a picture of one of the main characters and below it, write six quotations from the book. Two must describe him or her emotionally, two physically, and two more to show interests or actions central to the plot.	What happens in the novel? Draw and label a timeline of the events in the book.	Complete a SWBST (Somebody Wanted, But, So, Then) chart for all of the characters in your novel.
Response: Did you enjoy the book? Why or why not? Provide at least four examples from the book of things the author did well or did not do well.	**Creative:** *Choose only one:* ♦ Design a book cover, and be prepared to explain it. ♦ You are a movie director. Who would you cast in the roles of the main characters, and why? ♦ Write a new ending for this book.	**Write the Test:** Create a test based on your novel with an answer key. It must at least 25 questions in a variety of questioning formats (multiple choice or matching, fill-in the blanks, short answer).
Quotable quotes: Select at least four passages from a variety of places in the book and explain why they are significant.	**Conflict:** Find at least four conflicts within the novel (man vs. man, nature, self). Give evidence of each from the book.	**Title:** Why is the title of your book what it is? Please be sure to explain fully both the literal (surface level) and figurative (deeper level) meanings.

Gardner's Tic-Tac-Toe

There are several frameworks to use that incorporate current educational theory on differentiating learning styles, such as this Gardner's multiple intelligences tic-tac-toe (with a sample activity for each):

Linguistic: Make up a riddle about …	Bodily/Kinesthetic: Compare … to a sport or other activity.	Musical: Write a song with lyrics about …
Naturalist: Connect this to a plant or animal.	Student choice	Visual/Spatial: Create a picture that represents …
Interpersonal: Interview someone about …	Logical/ Mathematical: Develop a time line for …	Intrapersonal: Tell about a time when … was important to you.

For many more ideas on tasks to fit these learning styles, see the Gardner's list in Appendix 1.

Here is an example of such a grid for an earth science class on erosion:

Bodily/Kinesthetic	Interpersonal	Musical
Construct a 3-dimensional model of your choice of landform. Use the terms from the chapter to label and be prepared to explain your model, pointing out erosional, depositional, and biological aspects.	Design 10 survey questions about the effects of weather and other erosional agents. Ask at least six adults to respond. Analyze your results, and share a visual representation of your investigation process and conclusions.	Compose a song or rap about erosion, with some hand movements to go with it. Make sure the song is informative as well as fun. *or* Make a musical tape of songs or parts of songs representing all five natural erosional forces. Explain why you chose each.
Intrapersonal	**Logical/Mathematical**	**Visual/Spatial**
Propose a project or product that will show your understanding (or worries) about erosional forces. Get approval from me before you begin. Present it using some sort of technology (PowerPoint or digital photos?).	What erosional features are found in our county? Schedule a visit to the state park and speak with the naturalist. Prepare questions to ask and take notes and photos. Share the information you get visually.	Write a guided tour of an erosional landform. Make sure you sound like an expert on the topic. Choose some visuals (props, photos, or PowerPoint) as well as some good background music for your presentation.

Naturalist	Linguistic	Logical/Mathematical
With a parent or a partner, explore a river or stream in the area, using your senses and keeping a written (or picture) record of your exploration. Share the data and your impressions with the class in a format of your own choosing.	Write a newspaper (with illustrations) containing a different article on an incident involving each of the five natural agents of erosion. Include at least one advertisement as well.	Construct 10 mathematical story problems that show us information on erosion that you think is valuable to know. Hand them out, let us solve them, and explain the significance of the results to us.

Bloom's Tic-Tac-Toe

And perhaps instead of differentiating for learning styles, you might wish to provide choice of difficulty level. Here's a skeleton model for a grid based on Bloom's taxonomy:

Analyzing	Evaluating	Understanding
Creating	Applying	Analyzing
Evaluating	Remembering	Creating

Here is a brief explanation of the types of things to ask students to do in creating a grid using the preceding framework, starting with the lowest level of performance:

♦ *Remembering:* Ask students to list and describe content they remember, for example, using a KWL chart.

♦ *Understanding:* Students would demonstrate their comprehension of information by comparisons, explanations, paraphrasing, interpretations, predictions, and/or summaries of that information.

♦ *Applying:* This involves asking students to apply information to a real-life situation. They might classify, calculate, construct a diagram, or dramatize a concept.

♦ *Analyzing:* For analysis, they must break material into its constituent parts; determine how the parts relate to one another and to an overall structure or purpose; and then differentiate between different types to organize, order, compare, or explain them.

♦ *Creating:* A synthesis activity requires combining elements to form a coherent or functional whole; reorganizing elements into a new pattern or structure through generating, planning, or producing. This would most often use words like combine, plan, or compose.

♦ *Evaluating:* The highest level of Bloom's has students making judgments about the information based on specific criteria, using commands such as rank, assess, conclude, or critique.

Health Tic-Tac-Toe

Here is a really great physical education/health tic-tac-toe contributed by Shelly Barnes, a physical education instructor in Laurinburg, NC:

1. Collect: Facts about teens and obesity to be presented in class.	2. Teach the class different aerobic and anaerobic exercises they could be involved in.	3. Compare and contrast your pre–physical fitness results with your post–physical fitness results.
4. Determine your target heart rate (HR) for exercising including minimum HR and maximum HR.	5. Create a nutrition plan that would be more health for you and one you would enjoy sticking with.	6. Design a personal fitness plan to help you stay physically fit for life.
7. Survey your peers and determine how well teenagers eat nutritiously.	8. Calculate your body mass index (BMI) as well as your family's. Devise family strategies to improve fitness levels.	9. Predict how your fitness level will change over the course of the semester. Explain why?

Directions: Choose three activities from the tic-tac-toe menu. Must pick three that make tic-tac-toe.

List your choices: _____, _____, _____

Extra Credit: _____

Student's Signature:_____ Date:_____

In Appendix 1, there is a big chart of prompts to use in a Bloom's tic-tac-toe grid.

Bingo Assessments

These are the same concept as a tic-tac-toe grid, but instead of nine boxes, there are 25, five each in five horizontal rows, like a bingo grid. Students would then be asked to earn a *Bingo* (5 in a row, horizontally, vertically, or diagonally) for an A. These can be done over a period of weeks, and it is easy for students to see progress being made. They may submit assignments regularly at specified intervals, or as a packet, according to their agreement with the teacher. (Note: I usually limit students to two attempts to secure a space, and use a stamp on the grid to show them when they have successfully completed an activity.)

When I decide to award points for this, a Bingo (5 in a row) is an A; 4 is a B, 3 is a C, and 2 is a D. My students report that they appreciate having a wide choice of activities to do. I have observed that students seem more motivated and that their performance on the summative is better. Sometimes I have even used a bingo as the summative itself. One of my bingo grids, for a French unit on the family, is shown on the following page.

Homework Grid: The Family—French I

Vocabulary*	Speaking/ Listening*	Writing*	Technology*	Culture
Make a set of flash cards for all the words in this chapter.	Call my voicemail and leave me a message and a question.	Write a postcard or a letter about your family.	Print out a page about a French family that interests you that is either in French or English (or create one).	Look at a French work of art featuring a family& write a story, poem, rap, dance, or song about it.
Draw a picture illustrating chapter vocabulary and label all items.	Tape yourself speaking aloud (monologue or reading from text) and listen to it.	Draw a cartoon (or use one from a newspaper) with dialogue or descriptions for each cell.	Write a scavenger hunt on French families that uses at least 3 web sites, with questions to answer.	Write approximately half a page about a famous French family (see me if you need a suggestion!) (E).
Do a Memory Model for at least 4 vocabulary words. Make up several riddles involving vocabulary. *or*	Listen to a classmate tell you about his/ her family and write 5 sentences about what you heard, or draw a family tree.	Write a short story, skit, dialogue, poem or song about families, at least 10 lines/ sentences.	Do a Power Point or a trifold brochure on your family or a "dream" family. (E)	Have a family member help you draw a family tree, and teach them something about French families while you work on it together. @
Make a crossword, word search, or other game to practice vocabulary.	Do all the listening and speaking activities from the chapter.	Cut out a picture of a family & write me 6 sentences about it.	Play a game about families online, in French, from my web site. @	Write a short biography about an historical figure and his/ her family.
Teach some French to a friend, child, or family member. @	Memorize a poem, quote, or proverb about families. (OK the selection with me.)	Write out questions to interview someone about their family.	Create an invitation to a family party. On it, state which family member will bring different things to it.	Watch a French movie that I've approved, and write out a family tree showing the characters' relationships.

*All items in this column must be done using vocabulary and/or grammar from the *current* chapter.

@ Needs a parent or guardian's signature as verification.

All work must be done in French unless you see an (E) in the box.

If you have another idea for something not on the grid and which would require at least 15 minutes to do, see me for approval.

Bingo grids also can have only four rows. Here's one for biology:

Make a graphic organizer with facts about plants.	Do a diary entry or storyboard showing what daily life would be without plants.	Using a chart, poster or diagram, compare plant needs and part functions with those of a human body.	Make an audio or videotape interview with an organic plant.
Write or give a speech about the benefits of plants in daily life.	Survey the class about things they use that involve organic plants.	Construct a model of an organic plant, and label the parts.	Make a crossword about plants.
Suggest a new use for an organic plant product, and name your new process/item.	Make a picture book or a board game about plants.	Write a poem, rap, or song about organic plants.	Create a poster showing plants' effects on people.
Make a timeline of how a plant processes food and light.	Draw and label the parts and functions of the two kinds of plants.	Discover a new plant: Draw it, name it, and list its unusual features and uses.	Write a brochure or PowerPoint about the functions of the different parts of plants.

Role, Audience, Format, and Topic Assessments

Role, audience, format, and topic (RAFT) is a grid activity where students are given choices of role, audience, format, and topic. It is always based on unit objectives and standards and makes a writing assignment much easier for less-than-gifted students. Practically all RAFT writing is done from a fictional viewpoint. Here is an example of an RAFT assignment I use for a foods unit:

Role	Audience	Format	Topic
Cookbook writer	Cooks	Recipe	Instructions on food preparation
Chef	Customer	Menu	Detailed description of food preparation
Host/hostess	Servant	Dinner party plans	List foods (and amounts) to purchase, where to buy them, and other necessary preparations
Customer	Restaurant owner	Complaint	Problem with food and/or poor service
Travel writer	Reader wanting to travel	Recommendation	Good things to eat while, and what to avoid
Student overseas	Parents	Letter	Staying with a family, you describe a typical meal
Pick one of the above situations, pick up a checklist for that particular format, and use the Internet, Microsoft Publisher, and any other source to make your work look real.			

Here is a great web site that will help you design your own RAFT writing assessment for social studies, science, math, and more: http://www.writingfix.com/WAC/RAFT.htm.

Tiered Assessments

Tiered lessons, like many other teaching strategies, are also known under other names, including Layered Curriculum and Multiple Menu lessons. A tiered lesson begins with the presentation of a skill or concept in a whole group format, and then students are put into small groups (usually groups of three work best, in my opinion) that begin to explore this concept in a *tiered* manner, as follows.

There are four different ways to *tier* a lesson:

1. By resources
2. By outcome
3. By process
4. By product

Tiered assignments focus on students all learning same essential skills and understandings—but at different levels of complexity, abstractness, and open-endedness.

Teachers adjust assignments according to students' readiness or skill levels to challenge all students. Because most tiered lessons are written as trilevel (low, middle, high), it makes sense that the assessments for the end of a differentiated unit would be equally stratified. After practicing the skills at varied levels, with progress assessed formatively, the final product or test should be adjusted to the manner in which students learned the skills. All students are expected to demonstrate full proficiency for their levels.

If you are planning to give a standard book test, look at or write the test *before* you plan the tiered lessons and make sure the practice activities for each level are teaching the skills in the manner in which they must be demonstrated on the test. If students must write about a subject, all three tiered groups must do a written activity. If they must perform a physical task, they must practice that exact task.

Start with the lowest level performance, and design it first. The lowest level's expectation would be the standard or benchmark performance, with the other two levels expected to exceed that performance.

To increase the complexity of an assignment, ask students to:

♦ Add an unexpected element to the process or product: "What would happen if ..."

♦ Analyze the action or object

♦ Analyze an author's intent, style, or bias

♦ Apply the concept to other areas (especially a real world application)

♦ Argue against something that is generally accepted as true

♦ Combine several unrelated concepts or objects to create something new

♦ Compare and contrast two concepts, poems, or topics

♦ Critique something using a given set of standards

♦ Defend a piece of work he/she has completed

♦ Demonstrate higher-level thinking (Bloom's or Williams' taxonomy)

- ◆ Identify bias or prejudice in an argument
- ◆ Identify misconceptions
- ◆ Identify patterns or connections between two or more things
- ◆ Increase the number of variables that must be considered (incorporate more info)
- ◆ Look for other ways to define a problem
- ◆ Manipulate information rather than just echo it
- ◆ Negotiate the criteria to be used in evaluation
- ◆ Recount how they developed a particular concept or approach to a topic
- ◆ Select from several choices
- ◆ Use skill(s) in an unfamiliar situation
- ◆ Work independently
- ◆ Work with advanced resources

To reduce the complexity of an assignment:

You may still do all the levels of Bloom's, but you should be sure to do the following:

- ◆ Limit the number of variables for which students must account
- ◆ Limit the symbols students must interpret
- ◆ Suggest some possible items for use in the answer (i.e., theorems, a word bank of vocabulary)
- ◆ Provide a graphic organizer or other structure for the student answer

Several things should be done when tiering:

- ◆ Label teams neutrally: colors, items of clothing, or use key terms or concepts as group names.
- ◆ Be equally enthusiastic about every group's assignment.
- ◆ Take turns which level of activity is introduced first (don't always start with the basic one).
- ◆ All activities should be equally interesting and motivating.
- ◆ Unless you're tiering for learning preference, all groups' assignments should be equally active (no paper-and-pencil for one, while another does a skit or makes a video).
- ◆ All assignments should be fair in terms of the work involved. Think about the amount of work time involved, and be careful to make the time commitments as equal as possible.

If you are planning to give each tier group a different form of performance assessment, also pay careful attention to these considerations:

♦ Would students think each is comparable in terms of time and effort?

Stronger students shouldn't be asked to do more work just because they can. They will resent having to do something much more difficult for the same grade, and you'll hear from their parents as well. Think *separate, but equal* when choices are offered.

♦ Do options allow for a variety of learning styles, interests, prior knowledge, and/or readiness?

Don't despair at having to have several assessments; a variety of assessments is much less repetitive and boring to grade!

For most tiered lessons, the easiest summative assessment, if not using an actual text-generated test, would be to have students could select one of their practice activities to do, without books or reference materials, as a grade for that unit.

Learning Contracts

A type of differentiated assessment that usually includes formative and summative would require a written proposal by students that describes how they intend to display their knowledge, and how they would like it to be evaluated.

Why Use a Contract?

Because students

♦ develop ownership of what they are studying because they have input and some control.

♦ work at their own pace (within reason).

♦ work together with the teacher to agree on the terms of the contract. (It is not just student choice; the teacher has a considerable amount of input.)

Who Can Use a Contract?

This is a standard strategy for students who are compacting a unit. But students who fail to *compact out* of a specific unit might also choose to design a contract for learning, with the teacher allowing them to work on enrichment activities during the portions of class instruction that the teacher agrees the student has mastered and with a negotiated time for completion of the task.

How Does It Work?

For a learning contract, students choose what they will do (the depth and quantity of work), their work schedule (pace), and a topic that fulfills their individual needs and interests for an agreed-on grade. It must be noted, however, that the teacher still chooses the objectives to be addressed. The contract is in writing, with clear penalties for late or unsatisfactory performance and criteria, a rubric, for how it will be graded. (See the product sheet in the section on compacting in Chapter 5 for one that would be easy to adapt to this, or there is a free contract generator online at http://www.teach-nology.com/web_tools/contract/; although for secondary-level teaching you would need to totally modify the specifics from those provided.)

Steps in constructing learning contracts:

♦ Decide when students need whole group instruction, and when it is appropriate to allow students freedom.

♦ Introduce the unit as a whole group, to target the major concepts of the unit.

♦ Decide which students need learning contracts, and set them up: provide choices for students to research topics of their interest that are related to the unit.

♦ Require students to report their progress throughout the unit.

♦ Let parents know about the contracts.

One important step in contracting is to give students ownership in how their activity will be evaluated. Have them tell *you* what a good one looks like, sounds like, and so forth. This is advocated by many specialists (Wiggins, 1997) and in my experience, works really well. The contract should be mutually agreeable, and the students must be very clear on what *high-quality* work is. Incidentally, when setting up their criteria to show what's best, try to choose neutral words so there's no grade-specific feel to the evaluation.

Here are some suggestions (why not make them appropriate to your subject area?):

Bronze	Silver	Gold	Platinum
Attempted	Acceptable	Admirable	Awesome
Glass	Opal	Ruby	Diamond
Local	State	Regional	National
Larvae	Pupa	Cocoon	Butterfly
Peasant	Merchant	Noble	Pharaoh
Freshman	Sophomore	Junior	Senior
Page	Squire	Knight	Lord
Sour milk	Milk	Half-and-half	Cream
Jeans	Sport jacket	Suit	Tuxedo

Appendix 1 has a huge list of possible products they might propose in lieu of (or as a supplement to) unit activities: In my classes the most popular choices have been a student-written, short-answer or essay test; an oral or written report; a dramatic presentation; a mini-lesson; and a three-dimensional or other creative project. (Warning: Make sure they don't suggest something they can find in its entirety from another source. Every such proposal must have enough of an in-class component that you know it is the student's own work.)

Another suggestion: Students definitely need assistance to stay on track and complete the proposed project on time. Checklists help (see Appendix 3). So does a detailed step-by-step plan for completion, with one step to be completed by a specific day or week, agreed on and monitored by both the student and the teacher. A third method might be to stipulate what *working behavior* looks like during class, with statements such as, "Work without bothering other students" or "Avoid interrupting the teacher while he/she is teaching." I would suggest using all three documents. There should also be a statement in the contract about the consequences if the student does not fulfill any portion of the contract. usually, the student who breaks any portion of the agreement must abandon the alternative project and rejoin the class.)

"When the cook tastes the soup, that's formative. When the guests taste the soup, that's summative."

—Bob Stake, evaluation theorist

4

Summative Assessment: Putting Knowledge in Context

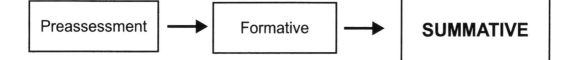

| Preassessment | → | Formative | → | **SUMMATIVE** |

Because there are so many types of summative assessment (often called simply *tests*), I am dividing the discussion of it between two chapters. I will not discuss the standardized test supplied by textbook companies, as several of the Show What You Know methods in the previous chapter adapt quite well to converting those to a more differentiated format.

Instead, Chapter 4 discusses a variety of performance-based assessments in which students display knowledge by using concepts and skills in an authentic context, often in ways other than written form. Chapter 5 discusses the most often used project style, written assessments (portfolios and projects), as well as some other options that give students an opportunity to be assessed in methods of their own choosing.

Authentic Assessment

As teachers, we should all be using practice activities as well as assessments that put knowledge and use of our subject area curriculum in context: Make students use it as they will/would have to in a real situation later in life. In such contexts, a multiple choice test will just not do; students must be in a hypothetical situation and asked to perform. Such an assessment is called an *authentic* or *alternative* or *direct* or *performance* assessment, and there are entire books written on this topic, including my book, *A Collection of Performance Tasks and Rubrics: Foreign Language*. The table on the next page compares and contrasts the selected-response (multiple choice) form of assessment with both authentic assessment and self-assessment.

The following text presents a short explanation of authentic or performance assessment.

Authentic Assessment Takes Multiple Forms

Authentic assessment asks students to analyze, apply, and sometimes synthesize what they have learned. Even though students may not be able to choose their own topics or formats, there are usually multiple acceptable routes toward constructing an acceptable product or performance. And, you as a teacher get a glimpse inside the students' heads in viewing these constructed response answers.

A Multiple Choice Assessment	A Performance Assessment	Self-Assessment
◆ Objective	◆ Presentational	◆ Reflective
◆ Knowledge focused	◆ Skills focused	◆ Analysis-focused
◆ No communication is necessary	◆ Involves teacher–student communication and support	◆ Student evaluates self, as many times as desired
◆ Teacher developed	◆ May be administered in a group format (skit, etc.)	◆ Student may have had input on criteria to be used
◆ One-time test with rapid results	◆ Assesses different learning styles and abilities	◆ May assess frequently over a long period of time
◆ Tests primarily recognition/recall	◆ Tests application of specific skills using a rubric or checklist	◆ Requires a performance or product (physical, oral, etc. often not based on reading)
	◆ More meaningful results	◆ Evaluates using a rubric or checklist
	◆ Perceived as more fair by students	◆ May be done in any format
		◆ No surprises in grade received; feedback before assessment is even presented to others
		◆ Contributes to perception of fairness
Drawbacks:	*Drawbacks:*	*Drawback:*
◆ Would be more difficult for students with poor reading/language skills	◆ Is more time-consuming to develop and grade	◆ Requires students to clearly understand rubric
◆ Allows guessing	◆ Feedback to student in terms of achievement of specific goals	
◆ Is difficult to construct well		
◆ Feedback in terms only of number of answers correct/types of questions missed		

Authentic Assessment Teaches Students Real Life Skills

Students shouldn't feel the need to ask, "When will we ever use this stuff?" Authentic assessments are close to how a student should apply the skill or knowledge in a real world situation. For example, in writing a report, the emphasis should be on doing something properly instead of how many sentences should be used; the skill is to know how when all aspects necessary have been included and discussed in sufficient detail, and in the correct form. Science papers, business letters, mathematical proofs, works of art, and other products obviously come in all different sizes/lengths. In an authentic assessment situation, the student's product should be allowed the same flexibility; quality rather than quantity is the goal. However, students should not be expected to achieve adult-level proficiency when they are supposed to be simply learning and improving their skills. Be careful not to structure your grading rubric with too-high expectations.

Evaluation of an Authentic Assessment Holds No Surprises for the Student

What might surprise you is that, in using an authentic assessment, teachers are encouraged to *teach to the test*. Students must learn how to perform well; and to help them, they should be shown models of good, mediocre, and bad performances. The student should also see the rubric for the task early in the process. Knowing what a good performance looks like and what specific expectations there are helps them to understand what sort of performance is necessary to succeed. Is this *cheating*? No; authentic assessments aren't the sort of thing that can be memorized and regurgitated, mimicked, or copied. Some skills they should be taught to practice and master are as follows:

- ◆ Gathering enough data
- ◆ Taking good notes
- ◆ Organizing the data logically
- ◆ Following protocols
- ◆ Explaining the data and organization of it to others
- ◆ Summarizing
- ◆ Weighing alternative strategies or viewpoints
- ◆ Generating hypotheses: What will happen if … why did it happen?
- ◆ Drawing conclusions, and checking the reasonableness of the conclusion

- Accounting for variables
- Predicting outcomes

Many of the preceding skills are in Marzano, Pickering, and Pollock's "seven strategies" and teachers should also take every opportunity to appeal to upper-level Bloom's strategies. Enough theory! Now let's discuss and see examples of various types of authentic assessments.

Product Assessments

After a prompt or series of prompts, students produce a product that shows their understanding of, and ability to use, a concept or skill. This takes more time to complete than a *select a response* type. Examples include the following:

- Short-answer essay questions
- *Show your work* answers
- Concept maps
- Graphic representation (e.g., Venn diagram)
- Journal-type/letter format response
- Checklists and inventories
- Stories or poems
- Research reports
- Extended journal responses
- Art exhibit
- Portfolio
- Newspaper
- Poster

There are many more examples, too, including most cooperative group projects.

As an example, in a math class, student responses to open-ended problems show how well a student thinks through a problem, a good indicator of how well he or she can use the required skills. In history or social studies, group projects such as a newspaper published as if it were for ancient Rome gives a good overview of how well the culture and concepts of that time period are being learned. Strengths and weaknesses of the performance are then analyzed by both the students and the teacher, and adjustments made for future instructional planning. For more examples, see the product list as well as the Gardner's-oriented one, both in Appendix 1.

An extra bonus in learning is gained when combining this type of assessment with a student-created evaluation instrument, as explained in Chapter 1. Designing their own checklist (for individual or classwide use) helps students think about skills they already have, skills they need to demonstrate, and what skills they may still need to acquire to complete a product and earn an *A*. Together, you may also wish to set a timeline and decide other questions:

♦ How will the items on a checklist be weighted?

♦ Will the product be the goal and the end of the unit?

♦ Or will the assessment be formative, checking progress, and being part of the grade in addition to the final product grade?

Any time students help define goals and monitor their own progress, they become more independent learners and more self-regulated, as they will be pleasing themselves as well as their peers and their teacher.

Performance-Based Assessments

In performance-based assessments (PBAs), after a prompt or an assignment or a presentation, students do something to show their understanding of the desired concepts and skills. Because performance-based assessments are complex, they are scored using rubrics indicating levels of performance on a variety of parameters. This type of assessment originated in the arts and in the apprenticeship systems, long ago. How can you evaluate a musician or singer's ability without hearing him or her perform? How can you judge the craftsmanship of a woodworker without seeing the furniture he or she has built? It is also impossible for those students to improve unless their instructor observes them doing a real task, provides feedback, monitors their use of the feedback, and adjusts the instruction, reteaching or trying a new approach. Using PBAs extends this practice to all subject areas.

Examples of School Tasks Used as PBAs

◆ Art work	◆ Inventions	◆ Notebooks	◆ Problems solved
◆ Athletic competition	◆ Internet transmissions	◆ Oral reports, debates, or discussions	◆ Puppet shows
◆ Collections	◆ Journals	◆ Original plays, stories, dances	◆ Reading selection
◆ Designs, cartoons, and drawings	◆ Letters	◆ Pantomimes	◆ Following a recipe
◆ Documentary reports	◆ Maps	◆ Plans for inventions, blueprints	◆ Scale models
◆ Experiments	◆ Model construction	◆ Poetry recitations	◆ Story illustrations
◆ Foreign language activities	◆ Musical compositions	◆ Photos	◆ Story boards
◆ Games	◆ Musical scores	◆ Performance: musical, dance, or dramatic (including exercise routines and fashion shows)	◆ Performances

The three most commonly used types of PBAs are performances, portfolios, and projects. The differences among these are often blurred by loose interpretations of these formats; but there are distinct differences, and I have chosen to put my discussion of portfolios in Chapter 5 and of E-portfolios in Chapter 6, as well as further examples of special projects in Chapter 5.

Pitfalls to avoid when doing a performance-based evaluation:

◆ Make sure the assessment matches how students learned and practiced the material. Don't have math students do multiple computations and then present them with word problems on the assessment. Don't have science students practice using *recipe labs,* which all produce the same result, and then ask them to demonstrate knowledge in an inquiry situation in which there are many possible results.

♦ Make sure the assessment doesn't need prerequisite skills that would compromise a student's ability to express mastery of a topic. Any of us who have had special needs or *English as a second language* students in our classes (*inclusion*) may have dealt with students who can orally discuss a topic well but are almost incapable of reading the question, because of poor reading skills, or of writing a grammatical, spelling-correct response. The same is true for a multimedia presentation, because students' experience with and skill in the format required profoundly affects the product and unduly influence the accuracy of the grade earned. Make sure the accommodations you make don't water down the mastery required, however. Some strategies might be to allow students to have someone read to them, dictate responses to an assistant, see/read less-subtle examples of a concept, break a task down into more manageable steps, or have additional time to study and review.

♦ Make sure the assessment isn't a *fluff* assessment. Posters that do not require students to explain concepts or procedures in detail, defining terms and using them correctly in a sentence, making a costume for a historical period; these are all time-consuming things that students detect immediately as fluff and resent doing.

Here's my suggestion for a really fun, interesting, and change-of-pace PBA: a mock trial.

Mock Trials

I think a mock trial would work for any subject area:

♦ Reenacting an historical trial

♦ Trying an historical figure for his/her actions/beliefs

♦ Trying a literary character (or writer) for his/her actions/beliefs

♦ Appealing current laws as they stand now (business law class or government)

♦ Accusing the legality of current events/actions such as civil wars, crimes, etc.

♦ Debating events or issues at the local level: school, classroom

I can see some easy science applications as well: Galileo on trial for theorizing a heliocentric solar system; a murder case involving radiation poisoning that could include evidence presented on radiation and its effects as well as proper safety procedures; and other forensic applications of laws of physics, gene manipulation, stem cells, and so forth.

A mock trial is generally based on either a conflict or dispute to be solved, or a crime that has allegedly been committed. Some are heavily scripted, as in a dramatic reenactment of an historical trial, or a foreign language skit that must use certain vocabulary words and structures in a fairly rigid sequence. Others have little or no script, in an attempt to simulate a real trial. The aim of mock trials, however, is not so much to imitate reality but to create a learning experience for students, and to make them think about the issues involved.

Take the following steps to prepare for the mock trial:

- Have a brief discussion about the purpose of trials and the procedure involved (see next step).

- Choose students (on a voluntary basis is preferable) to play the defendant (if a crime) or the petitioner and defendant (if a conflict or dispute), a judge and a bailiff, attorneys (more than one is preferable as there is a considerable amount of research and speaking involved) as well as witnesses, a jury, and even court reporters (print, radio, and television).

- Give students research and preparation time. If possible, bring in some legal professionals to advise them. During this time, jurors might explore the role of the jury, the historical development of the jury system, and other topics related to their role. The judge (and bailiff) should research courtroom procedures, and the judge should also become familiar with current law regarding issues such as the one being brought to trial. Witnesses should be prepared to testify about key ideas regarding the topic and help manufacture *evidence* to be used, if possible. The attorneys must develop opening and closing statements as well as questions for their own witnesses and questions to cross-examine witnesses for the other side.

The trial could also be organized using a RAFT (role, audience, format, topic) format. In this situation, each person has a role, an audience, a format, and a topic to guide his/her performance (see Chapter 3 for examples of RAFT structures).

When preparations have been completed, arrange the classroom into a courtroom. The trial itself usually has a realistic but simplified set of steps:

- The calling of the case by the bailiff: "All rise. The Court of _____ is now in session, Honorable Judge _____ presiding."

- Opening statements from the attorneys, with the prosecutor first and then the defense, each stating what they will try to prove.

- Prosecution's or plaintiff's case: Witnesses testify one by one and evidence is introduced. Each witness may be cross-examined (questioned so as to break down or discredit the story) by the defense attorneys.

- ◆ Defendant's case: Witnesses are questioned (direct examination) by the defendant's attorneys, and cross-examined by the prosecution or plaintiff's attorneys.

- ◆ Closing statements: One speaker for each side reviews the testimony and evidence presented and asks for a decision in favor of his or her side of the issue.

- ◆ Jury instructions: The judge explains the law on this topic to the jury, telling them what to consider in weighing the evidence to make their decision (i.e., the prosecution must prove guilt in a criminal case).

- ◆ The jury must reach a unanimous decision, and announce it to the class.

- ◆ The judge may pass sentence and, if guilt is determined, suggest a penalty of some sort (optional).

Mock trials are real attention grabbers that take advantage of student interest in various aspects, involve volunteers creatively, and still deliver educational information. In addition, it should be a nonthreatening exercise with plenty of time for a debriefing afterward to emphasize key points in the information delivered. All in all, they are fun and a learning experience as well as an assessment. Students like them and, in my experience, remember them fondly, as well as the issues and ideas involved.

More assessment methods that involve placing things in context are in the following sections.

Personalized Assessment

Some drivers may prefer to race down the highway, whereas others meander along the scenic route. Both drivers reach the same place. Students too may prefer different paths toward a learning goal, but they can all achieve the same understanding. So now I will just remind you of previously discussed, personalized assessments from Chapter 3: the students who chose their own vocabulary words to be tested on and wrote the quiz they would later take; students who proposed a project, outlined how they would accomplish it, and suggested criteria for its evaluation; or those on a WebQuest (see Chapter 6) whose search led them in different directions and to different end results. All these students would have unique content and should be tested in a unique manner. Allowing them to determine the manner of testing is also a form of empowerment.

One more way to personalize, however, is called a *focus on growth* assessment. Using your classroom observations, student scores on assignments, and comments made by the student on self-assessment questions and by partners in various groups, you can compile a sort of report card or update to give the student, using a spreadsheet, a chart, or whatever method you find easiest. You choose what sort of growth to chart; depending on the student, you can keep track of things like work handed in on time, test scores, how many times he or she contributes to class discussion, evaluations by group members of his or her helpfulness, or whatever behavior you'd like to reinforce. If the student knows you notice effort as well as success, and that classmates approve or disapprove of his or her behavior, it may make a difference.

At the school-system level, this is now being called *value-added* assessment, with a focus on growth over a longitudinal period. This comparison of previous assessment scores with more recent ones has the double advantage of documenting that progress *has* taken place as well as also eliminating the influence of student background characteristics (e.g., poor reading skills or a turbulent home environment) over which teachers have little or no control and that tend to bias test results. The Koalaty Kids project, a nationally recognized program, does just this. Check out this program on its web site: http://www.asq.org/edu/kkid/index.html/.

Partner and Group Testing

You might also consider allowing students to choose if they wish to be tested alone, with a partner or in small groups. Each person should still receive an individual grade, but for some students, the thought of an exam (especially an oral one) one-on-one with a teacher is extremely frightening, and having a buddy along for moral support could result in a better performance. This potential for enhancing a sense of partnership and trust between students, as well as between student and teacher, can offset quite a few of the negative attitudes students hold toward other forms of assessment.

Remember, once again, brain research that tells us that it is wise to recreate the learning situation when assessing. If this material was learned and practiced with a partner, or with the whole class interacting with the teacher, simply having a partner would allow students to more closely simulate the learning situation, and the student will have an easier time accessing what was learned.

Also, and especially if you have large classes, working with groups to test has other benefits: It somehow seems easier to manage five groups of six rather than 30 individuals in terms of movement, and the group tests could be spread out over several class periods as well. As for frequency of use, that's up to you; several math teachers in my building do this for every unit, but not all units or subject areas may lend themselves to this sort of test.

What does a group test look like? Usually, everyone in the group gets the same test paper. Note: these are not multiple choice or true/false tests; these are tests in which students generate compositions, graphics, sentences, respond to readings, and so forth in which there may be more than one correct answer (e.g., comparing and/or discussing differing opinions on a topic, two wars or time periods, a possible application for an equation to a novel situation, and so on). Students in a group can work separately or talk to each other but all write their own answers. Then you have two options: Let the group decide whose paper to turn in as their grade, or you can randomly choose one student (biggest shoe size, closest birthday, or whatever) to hand in his or her paper with the group's names on it.

If that is too nontraditional for you, here are some alternatives that you might consider the following:

♦ Give the test individually and then, the last 2 minutes or so, let them talk to anyone they want. One of my math colleagues (who won't let me use her name) allows students to collaborate for the first 10 minutes, and then they must finish the test individually. She says they quickly scan through the test and have a partner reteach or refresh their knowledge on how to solve the problem(s) that seem most difficult to them. This is a good peer-teaching dynamic, even at a very late hour in the learning process. She also sometimes gives a two-part test. One part may be done in small *pod* groups who normally work together daily, and becomes about 35% of the test grade. The other portion is a standard individual test. Because her classes are generally made up of low-achieving and special needs students, she reports that this method starts them off with confidence that at least they have that part of the test (and shows groups that didn't do much work together before the value of increased collaboration before the next test), and, again, allows for some last-minute learning opportunities.

♦ Give students a very short time period before the test to talk and write down anything they want, and allow them to use those notes during the test.

♦ Give a class grade: The whole class can talk to each other, and all need to write. Then, collect the tests and put them in a pile. Correct only the first response on the first test paper, the second on the second paper, and so on. Everyone in the class gets the final grade, and the class will make sure the *slackers* work, because it affects their grade. More on this strategy may be found by looking under the term *round robin*. I sometimes do this when everyone did rather poorly on a test, regiving the same test or a similar one, and averaging the new grade with the previous one.

This method encourages the student-helping-student dynamic that brain research says is so good for long-term memory storage.

Summary

Authentic assessment is product- and performance-oriented, and may be done in a variety of formats: individual as well as collaborative (small group, large group). Authentic assessments ask students to perform in a real-world situation or format, analyze their performance, and reflect on it. The use of rubrics in this form of assessment enables students to understand the skills and criteria before the assessment begins, to self-evaluate their product before handing it in, and to quickly receive feedback on areas that have improved, or still need improvement.

5

Summative Assessment: Using Variety

As we agreed very early in this book, all students are not alike. Each has a unique variety of strengths and weaknesses which call for a unique assessment. Offering a choice of appropriate ways to assess a unit is what would be best if the desired outcome is for the student to be able to choose and adapt summative activities in order to be successful. This chapter discusses several methods of assessment that provide structured and easy-to-evaluate yet still distinctly different results for each student.

Several Arguments for Using Variety

♦ Students should not always be assessed in the same manner. Brain research and personal observation should teach us that students have different learning styles. We need to give students more than one opportunity to display mastery of the material learned.

♦ Studies have shown you probably prefer (and write) tests that appeal to your own learning style. If you assess in only one way, this favors students with that particular learning style only.

♦ Anyone with a basic knowledge of scientific procedure knows that if an experiment is to be valid, it needs to be done multiple times, and over a period of time, and varying small elements of the procedure. What is true for experimental design is also true for instructional design.

♦ In my classroom I often observe that a student who knows something one day may or may not know it on a later date. Students may have test anxiety, be getting ill, have skipped breakfast or lunch, or have something personal going on in their life that more than trumps anything happening in my classroom. Allowing them more than one opportunity to show me their best effort just makes sense.

♦ Secondary-level students aren't adults yet, and it's not really developmentally appropriate to hold them to adult standards. Just because the real world doesn't often allow things to be redone in a second attempt at mastery doesn't mean that students shouldn't redo assignments. Taking an assignment and perfecting it, like a cook with a favorite recipe, reflecting and adjusting the product until it is the best it can be, is an essential element of the portfolio, one of the strategies discussed in this chapter.

For all these reasons, and more, teachers should use a variety of approaches to the following aspects of assessment:

♦ Pacing

♦ Structuring

♦ Learner independence

♦ Learning task

♦ Abstractness or concreteness

♦ Depth and complexity.

This chapter explores strategies that allow students to really *show what they know*.

Knowledge Mapping

Knowledge mapping is a year-long project, a strategy used by many businesses, so teaching this to students might actually be teaching them a skill to use on a future job as well as in your classroom. It has three parts to track the acquisition and loss of information and knowledge.

1. Survey

2. Audit

3. Synthesis

The user explores his or her own competencies and skills as well as those of others.

It is actually a sort of graphic, like a mind map, that is kept from the beginning of the year to the end, which shows them that they are adding to their knowledge. Students list what they know on the first day they begin to make the map, and add information to it as the class continues; therefore they chart and see their own growth. I know that every time my students master a new concept, I just push them to another new concept. This strategy helps them take stock of how far they have come since they began the class and is also available at semester exam time as a good listing of what might be on the test as well as their own strengths and weaknesses.

Types of things for students to think of when drawing a knowledge map:

♦ What type of knowledge or skill is needed?

♦ Where can that knowledge be found?

♦ Who can help? Who do you go to when you have a problem?

♦ What would make your work easier?

♦ What happens when you are finished?

If you have computers available, there is a free tutorial that shows what a knowledge map looks like, and how it works: http://www.thebrain.com/#-56/ (JJanuary 2008). I have found this to be an option that my students with individualized education programs (IEPs, or special needs) especially enjoy having as an option they can use, because it helps them easily organize and display what they know.

Flex Fund

Think about setting aside a certain number of points for each grading period in a *Flex Fund*. My insurance offers a Flex Fund-like discretionary funding program where I can tailor my insurance to meet my personal needs. In a classroom Flex Fund, students may choose how they would like to earn their Flex Fund points, which usually are assigned to be the equivalent of one unit test grade, or as a replacement for a project: variety in action, coupled with student choice. Flex Funds are also good for taking up extra time students may have when finishing a project early, an extension of learning for all students, or as another *mental touch* on subject material in the evening, on *off days* for those of us with an alternating-day schedule, or over a long weekend or vacation period. You choose what types of activities they may use for Flex Fund points. Options may include the following:

Class Participation

Give students a rubric that explains what *good* participation is. Here is a sample:

Criteria	Never	Sometimes	Always
Productive	0	3	4
Well-timed	0	2	4

Prepared	0	2	4
Accurate	0	4	8

Other categories to consider adding to this rubric might be listens well to others, attendance, and nondisruptive behavior (sounds, gestures, and comments). You also should list (or have students help you list) activities that would apply: reading aloud, asking productive questions, offering answers, interpretations or observations, participating in online blogs or mentor experiences, after school activities, and so on.

Close-ups

A *close-up* is an in-depth investigation of a subject only touched on in class or in the book. It may involve an image or illustration, a list of facts or examples (e.g., of a grammar point or a scientific theorem and its exceptions), a news article, or other product. Students are expected to present their results to classmates in written or oral form or as a display, so everyone benefits from their research. Having student experts on chapter topics is a definite bonus! (PS: Remember to always ensure that these investigations involve some higher-level thinking elements to extend learning, not just a rote report.)

Leadership

Students could earn leadership points by leading a group, maintaining order and focus in the group or class, or tutoring another student.

Notebook Grades

Do you check and grade notebooks? Some teachers have students keep precise notebooks, divided into sections such as vocabulary, rough drafts, class notes, end-of-chapter questions, chapter outlines, video worksheets, and so on. Then they give grades based on whether all student papers are in the notebook, organizational skills, neatness and completeness of work, whether mistakes have been corrected on all papers, whether notes have been rewritten and/or key information highlighted, and so forth.

Other teachers actually give notebook quizzes with questions (described during the early weeks of the school year) about vocabulary words, about graded work, about daily or chapter objectives, about handouts, or about other activities done in class. If the notebook is properly maintained, students should be able to get 100% on the quiz.

Optional Test Grades

With *optional test grades,* a student could choose to drop a low test score or double a high one. He or she could also take an optional review test or a test over a supplementary topic on which he or she has done some research or a report.

Work With a Tutor

Students can work with a tutor or show other evidence of test preparation activity. Work must be documented: with whom, what was studied, where, and for how long.

Special Projects

Special projects would be a written, oral, or visual report on supplementary readings (magazines, news articles, Internet sites, or films, for example), interviews, displays or models for the classroom, graphic organizers or review games, or other ideas students may propose. Be careful that these are not things they may simply *lift* from the Internet. These projects could be a good way for students to make connections with other subject areas, which enhance long-term learning: a book report on *Les Miserables* done for your class and English class, a report on a famous artist or a copy of a famous painting for art (or for history if the art shows a famous event), and so on.

Charting Growth

Charting growth may involve any self-evaluation that would show an increase of knowledge. Examples include using a knowledge map as discussed in the previous section, doing the L part of a KWL (know, want to know, and learned), and working on a portfolio-type task.

Flex Fund Sample

There are quite a few examples on the Internet of assessments of this type, but using a wide variety of names, including *choice list, participation buffet, assignment options, and others.* Here is an example of a Flex Fund in which I've combined elements from several of the available examples. All the Flex Funds I found were made up of entirely written work, with the exception of a portfolio conference (based on written work), so I've tried to include some options for differentiation of styles, unlike the ones I found on the Internet.

Flex Fund Options List

Maximum possible: 100 points

- ♦ If you wish to use this option, at least 40 points must be completed before halfway through the grading period, which is _____.
- ♦ Keep track of your Fund Points on the half sheet provided.
- ♦ All points/work must be submitted by the Friday before final exams.

Option 1: Homework packets 20 points per unit, maximum of 3. These are due on the day of the test over the unit, and must:

- ♦ be fully and *neatly* done.
- ♦ be clearly labeled for section, page, and assignment number.
- ♦ show clear evidence that you have checked its accuracy.

Option 2: Work with a tutor or partner(s) 10 points each, maximum of 6.

- ♦ You may not submit more than 2 sessions for any given week.
- ♦ Your meeting must last at least ½ an hour, be documented on a Help Session sheet, and be signed by your partner and an adult (parent or member of school staff).

Option 3: Notebook grade 10 points each, max. depends on number of tests. Due on the day of the unit test, before the test begins. You must show your preparation for the test in at least three of these ways:

- ♦ A clear outline of the information in the unit
- ♦ A list of key terms/ideas
- ♦ Cornell notes for the unit, with all questions answered
- ♦ A collection of *all* unit assignments, corrected and with key concepts starred or highlighted
- ♦ A study plan, with a description of how well you followed it
- ♦ Predictions of questions that you think will be asked on the test

Option 4: Test analysis 15 points each, maximum of 4. This must be turned in within *one* week of getting the test back. Must include the following:

- ♦ What went right or wrong with the test
- ♦ An analysis of work/study habits that helped or didn't help
- ♦ List of sections in the book that cover the portions you had difficulty with, with at least one activity from that section either explained or reworked correctly

Option 5: Leadership 5 points each, maximum 3 per grading period. You may show leadership in any of the following ways:

♦ Tutor a classmate (see Option 2)

♦ Lead a group (project, group reading, conversation); does *not* include teams for games

♦ Maintain order or focus during class, assisting teacher

Option 6a: Portfolio, 20 points. These are due during the week before finals. It must have *all* materials from class: handouts, homework and other assignments. It must be

♦ organized in a way that makes sense to you. *Note:* You must to explain this method to me in a one-on-one review of your portfolio.

♦ accompanied by a brief paper in which you tell the following:

  • things you are proud of.

  • things you still need work on.

  • what you liked most or least.

Option 6b: Reflective Piece, 15 points; no more than 3. Taking time to think about what you've learned, what works best for you to learn well, changes you've made or could make, is the mark of a good student. This is your chance to share ideas as well as discuss and communicate experiences. This may be in a variety of formats:

♦ A paper

♦ A poster

♦ A PowerPoint (on disc)

♦ A taped (audio or video) discussion

♦ Other format suggested by student

Option 7: Spin-off 15 points (25 points if presented to class); maximum 2.

♦ Do some additional research on a topic that was mentioned but not discussed in detail, or one that is related and that you'd like to know more about. Remember that it cannot be just lifted from the Internet but must be in your own words (school plagiarism policy applies!).

♦ May be presented visually (copy for everyone in class, PowerPoint, poster, etc.) or orally (brief speech) for an additional 10 points. To earn these 10 points, it must be done *during* the unit that contains this topic, not after the unit is completed.

(Continues on next page.)

★ ★

FLEX FUND FOR:

_____ (Name)

List total points: _____ Option 1 (max 60)
                       _____ Option 2 (max 60)
                       _____ Option 3 (max varies)
                       _____ Option 4 (max 60)
                       _____ Option 5 (max 20)
                       _____ Option 6 (max 45)
                       _____ Option 7 (max 50)

   TOTAL: _____ points (you may only use 100 points)

How I'd like to use my points:

◆━━━━━━━━━━━━━━━━━━━━━━━━━━━━━━◆

HELP SESSION SHEET: *Must be submitted within one week of date of meeting*

Name _____

Met with: _____

Date: _____

   From _____ to _____   Total minutes: _____

Description of what worked on/discussed:

Further plans:

Signature of helper(s): _____

Signature of adult: _____

Compacting

Imagine yourself stuck in traffic and anxious to move ahead, scanning the area for an alternative route. Learners who already have a significant amount of knowledge of a particular subject may feel just as bored and frustrated. Providing an alternative route for these advanced learners may avoid such negative feelings.

Compacting may defined as determining which students already have a good understanding of a given concept and then giving those students choices of (usually independent) activities for their class time while the others are brought *up to speed* by the teacher (a longer definition may be found in Appendix 2).

There are two basic types of compacting:

1. *Basic Skills Compacting.* After a diagnostic test of skills such as spelling, math computation, or reading, students who score well may skip the practice activities and do a compacting activity.

2. *Content Compacting.* Students determined to have sufficient knowledge of topics in social studies, science, health, physical education, literature, math applications, and problem-solving would be offered the option of compacting for that unit only. The study by Reis and colleagues (1993) found that "approximately 40% to 50% of traditional classroom material could be eliminated for targeted students in one of more of the following content areas: mathematics, language arts, science, and social studies" and that math used compacting most often, followed by the others in the same order as written preceding. In addition, they found that assessment results after compacting showed no difference between compacted and control groups in terms of skills like reading, spelling and math computation. The five steps to successful compacting are described in the following sections.

Step 1: Identify Goals and Outcomes

Identify the goals and outcomes of the unit and design the final assessment. (This is what one would do when beginning any unit, of course!) Decide what score would indicate mastery of this material. Many teachers use 80% on a preassessment as an indication of mastery (Reis et al., 1998).

Step 2: Identify Compacting Candidates

Identify students who are good candidates for compacting. Student behaviors that signal that compacting would be a good alternative:

- ♦ Creates games, puzzles or other diversionary tasks for him- or herself while waiting for slower students to finish
- ♦ Does work well and correctly
- ♦ Expresses interest in pursuing related topics
- ♦ Seems to have some advanced familiarity with the material
- ♦ Shows a high level of motivation

Step 3: Pretesting

After an introductory lesson (don't skip that step!!), pretest all students to positively identify those who already have mastery of the subject. Most often, this is done by administering the final assessment (or one very like it), often referred to as a *skills inventory*, as a diagnostic tool. Students who score well (a score of 80% to 90%, according to my informal survey of schools that use compacting) are identified as candidates for compacting.

Step 4: Enrichment

Students who *compact out* are then physically excused from much of the regular instructional time to work on material that is more meaningful to them; however, compacted students still have regular instructional time with the teacher. The compacting activities must still address the content studied and standards addressed, yet they should be more sophisticated, specialized, and/or challenging.

The teacher and student choose accelerated or enrichment *choice* activities for the student to do while the other students master the concept. If there is only one student, that student will still be included in instructional time rather than isolate him/her (such as doing whole class writing, manipulative or technology activities), but if small groups are possible, students may be sent other places under the supervision of a mentor or the media service personnel to work on enrichment activities. Enrichment may include but is not limited to:

- ♦ A more complex investigation of unit content
- ♦ A creative/original project and product
- ♦ An in-depth investigation of a self-selected topic in the current content area

Selecting an Appropriate Activity

The first step in selecting an appropriate activity might be to administer an Interest Survey like that on the foillowing page.

Interest Survey

Please check all the responses that apply to you:

Would you enjoy...?	Yes, I would	No, I wouldn't	I might enjoy it	I've done this
Acting in a theatrical production				
Being a photographer				
Being involved in a community project				
Belonging to an environmental group				
Belonging to an astronomy club				
Conducting an experiment				
Creating a comic strip				
Designing a building				
Designing costumes or furniture				
Developing and managing a computer bulletin board				
Developing your own photos				
Inventing something				
Investigating the stock market				
Keeping a personal journal or diary				
Learning a handicraft				
Organic gardening				

(Continues on next page.)

Would you enjoy...?	Yes, I would	No, I wouldn't	I might enjoy it	I've done this
Painting or sketching people, objects, or landscapes				
Publishing something you've written				
Repairing a car or appliance				
Starting a musical group (vocal or instrumental)				
Starting a school newspaper				
Starting a new club or team				
Starting your own business				
Visiting a museum or historical site				
Volunteering time for charity				
Working on a political campaign				

You could also determine a student's interests by asking one or more of the following questions:

- ◆ Design the perfect class for your high school. What would it be called, and what would be taught?

- ◆ You have received some money but must spend it on a field trip from school. Where would you go? List at least two ideas, telling why you'd want to go there and what you would do there.

- ◆ You are going to prepare a time capsule of personal possessions that represent you. What would you put in the capsule, and why?

- ◆ If you could interview anyone you admire, past or present, who would it be? What would you ask him or her?

- ◆ You are given the chance to travel back in time: What time period would you go to, and who would you meet there? What would you like to do?

- ◆ You are going to compete in three events, individual or group performance. What would you be competing in? (Note: these events could be physical or knowledge-oriented.)

- ◆ You have designed a computer program. Describe the program.

- ◆ List five books or magazines you enjoy, with your favorite first.

- ◆ You've just published your first book. What is the title? What is the book's subject?

- ◆ Briefly describe any collections you have, or tell what you'd like to collect if you had the time and money to do so.

- ◆ You are going to join a job mentoring program. List three occupations you are interested in.

- ◆ You have the opportunity to work with elected officials on issues of importance. What issues do you think need to be addressed, and why?

- ◆ You are going to participate in the debate. What is the topic, and which side would you take?

- ◆ You are a photographer and you have one picture left on your camera. What will you take a picture of, and why?

- ◆ You are going to make a movie! Check the three types you'd consider doing:

☐ Adventure	☐ Documentary	☐ Historical	☐ Science fiction
☐ Biography	☐ Drama	☐ Horror	☐ Teen
☐ Classic	☐ Fantasy	☐ Musical	☐ Travel
☐ Comedy	☐ Foreign	☐ Mystery	☐ Other: _____

♦ You are attending a science conference. Sign up for your first, second, and third choices of seminar:

☐ Astronomy	☐ Geology	☐ Scientific research
☐ Ecology	☐ Health issues for teens	☐ Toxic waste
☐ Endangered species	☐ Medicine and medical issues	☐ Volcanoes
☐ Entomology	☐ Meteorology	☐ Other: _____
☐ Environmental issues	☐ Nuclear energy issues	
☐ Forensics	☐ Rain forests	
☐ Genetic engineering	☐ Robotics	

♦ You'll be working on the staff of a major newspaper/television news program. What topic would you specialize in? Check your top three choices:

☐ National events	☐ Movie reviews	☐ Celebrity news
☐ International events	☐ Music	☐ Crossword puzzles
☐ Local news	☐ Book reviews	☐ Home improvement
☐ Business	☐ Travel	☐ Personal advice
☐ Editorials	☐ Fashion	☐ Children's page
☐ Political commentary	☐ Food	☐ Consumer reports
☐ Political cartoons	☐ Advice	☐ Horoscopes
☐ Sports	☐ Humor/cartoons	☐ Other: _____

You could also give the student a SCAMPER sheet to help them find a new *twist* on the topic of study, and which would interest them enough to inspire some investigation or experimentation. SCAMPER is a brainstorming strategy and an acronym explained in the following:

Content Area: _____

Substitute	Who else? What else? Another place? Another time? Different materials?	Write your idea here:
Combine	Combine purpose? Ideas? Materials? Processes? People or products?	
Adapt	What is similar? What other ideas does this suggest? What part could I change or exchange?	
Modify Minimize Magnify	Could this be larger, stronger or multiplied? Could this be smaller, slower or split up? Could the color, motion, sound, form, shape or use be changed?	
Put to another use	Who or what else might be able to use it? What is a new way to use it?	
Eliminate	What if parts were subtracted or reduced? What if this didn't exist?	
Reverse Rearrange	What could this be with another layout? Another sequence?	

There's a good tutorial on this process at http://www.brainstorming.co.uk/tutorials/scampertutorial.html/ (January 21, 2008).

Managing the Compacting Situation

After selecting and agreeing on an alternative activity, teachers and compacting students should discuss behavioral expectations and sign some sort of plan or contract regarding their alternative assignments. The students should also be informed at the onset how their chosen activity will be evaluated.

WARNING: It is very important to use some sort of record to keep track of the progress of the students. You can have students use the student activity log (p. 85), project planner and checklist (p. 86) or the compacting sheet following (p. 87). The student activity log is particularly useful if you are recording grades chronologically (see Chapter 7), as you would want students to keep a daily activity log or journal.

Student Activity Log

Student _____

Project _____

Date	What did you do?	What will you do tomorrow? What help will you need?

Project Planner

Name(s): _____

TOPIC & QUESTIONS   Due date: _____

Specific topic_____

Specific questions to be answered (who/what/why/where/when):

_____

_____

(may go on attached sheet)

RESOURCES (at least 3)   Due date: _____

Print:_____

_____

Internet:_____

_____

Other:_____

PRODUCT DESCRIPTION   Due date: _____

I/we'll be doing the following:

_____

CHECKLIST   Due date: _____

You must complete the checklist for your type of project, and have a classmate fill out the checklist for you, too.

SHARING   Due date: _____

Here's how I plan to share my project with the class:

_____ display____ presentation   Details:

EVALUATION FORM   Due date:_____

Complete the Reflection form.

Compacting Form

Area above asterisks to be completed by student and OK'd by teacher before beginning!

Student Name: _____

Unit compacted: _____

Name/choice of project: _____

Resources needed:

Steps in project:

* *

Criteria for quality work:

_____ Checklist completed

_____ Self-evaluation completed

Method for sharing:

_____ Display _____ Presentation

Due date:_____

Step 5: Final Assessment

At the end of a compacted unit, all students take the final assessment, even those who compacted out of the unit (who were, after all, still investigating, practicing and/or evaluating the content and standards connected to the curriculum for the unit being taught).

Compacting Examples

Math

Students could choose to investigate any of the following topics:

- ♦ Probability of events and statistics
- ♦ Logical thinking

Science

The following topics were supplied by colleagues:

- ♦ Students who already understand photosynthesis might be given a lab assignment in which they must develop and test hypotheses related to the topic.

- ♦ Small groups can prepare and debate issues surrounding the origin of the universe.

- ♦ In earth science students could pursue interests such as classifying rocks or carbon dating.

- ♦ A student developed a plan for researching family traits and for learning about genetics, making a poster of his family tree (with graphics representing genetic traits) to present to the class.

Social Studies

- ♦ Explore the discoveries and inventions that have changed thinking and history. Some examples include maps, mapmaking, and their role in exploration; photography and the printing press and their ability to preserve the past, the railroads and their ability to bridge people and continents; telescopes and their ability to see into the past and future.

Spin-Offs

A term often used in science (and other subject areas) for the sort of independent study the advanced students do when compacting is an *orbital* or *spin off* to a topic of their own interest yet related to the subject being taught to the class at that time. Again, you will want students to fill out a form:

Spin-Off

Name: _____

Unit: _____

Specific topic:_____

What key ideas from the unit will you include?

List the steps you will take to complete the unit:

   1. _____

   2. _____

   3. _____

   4. _____

What resources do you plan to consult?

How long will this take? (estimate) _____

How will you share this?

Evaluation checklist: create a checklist of important components for your product:

   ☐ _____
   ☐ _____
   ☐ _____
   ☐ _____
   ☐ _____
   ☐ _____
   ☐ _____
   ☐ _____

Some Final Comments on Compacting

Most students will not compact out of all units. Each will have his or her own areas of strength and also a learning style that may connect naturally with some topics and not as fully with others.

Classrooms using compacting will differ, even if teaching the same topic. The numbers of compacting students may vary. Management styles may vary: Some teachers prefer using individualized folders for all students (eliminating the look of special treatment) with remedial activities in some and enrichment ones in others. Some classrooms have learning centers or games areas for all students who show an understanding of that day's lesson, skill, or concept.

Warnings: There must be a reward to the more advanced students, either a higher grade or less homework, for example, or there is no incentive to take advantage of compacting. There must also be some student choice involved in the interest of promoting the idea that allowing compacting is *fair* to all students.

Portfolios

Besides being a visible manifestation of what a student can do, how he or she practices it, how much growth has occurred in learning, and how it is assessed and evaluated by both the teacher and the student, a portfolio is a process, as well as a destination. Students have a natural tendency to save work (all those notebooks stuffed full of crinkled papers and handouts!) and this strategy takes advantage of that. Portfolios are an effective way to get them to take a second look at their work and think about how they could improve as well as a record of what they have achieved. It is also a way to show all the variety that students get in your classroom.

This is obviously a clear departure from the old *write, hand in, and forget* behavior in which students consider first drafts to be final products. A portfolio is a purposeful collection of student work that tells the story of a student's efforts, progress, or achievement in a given area over a period of time. A well-designed portfolio system can accomplish several important purposes: motivate students; provide explicit examples to parents, teachers, and others of what students know and are able to do; allows students to chart their growth over time and to self-assess their progress; and encourages students to engage in self-reflection.

Research shows that students at all levels see assessment as something that is done to them by someone else. Beyond percent correct, assigned letter grades, and grammatical or spelling errors, many students have little knowledge of what is involved in evaluating their work. Portfolios can provide structure and practice for involving students in developing and understanding criteria for good efforts, in coming to see the criteria as their own, and in applying the criteria to their own and other students' work.

Because portfolios are longitudinal (examining work over a period of time) and show the *big picture* of student development, this method is an extremely fair method of determining a student's grade compared to a single-sampling method such as a unit test or quiz. An assessment of student mastery based on examination of a portfolio is not only more valid, but also more effective.

When assigning a portfolio, consider the following issues:

♦ *What will it look like?* There must be a physical description given (what documents are used and how they are stored) as well as a conceptual structure (work around a theme such as best work, celebration, showcase, representative, or chronological). A portfolio is a flexible *chameleon* of an assessment. It can be as simple as a folder of collected work, or it can be a multimedia (including electronic, auditory, or nonpaper artifacts) or even a multiyear presentation of samples of student learning over time.

♦ *What goes in?* To make this decision, numerous other questions must be addressed: What kinds of evidence will best show student progress toward learning goals? Will the portfolio contain best work only, a progressive record of student growth, or both? If you want to show growth, include student work from various times during the period. To show best learning, have them choose what they consider to be their best effort. *Not all work goes into a portfolio!*

The following types of materials are often included in a portfolio:

• Writing samples such as journal entries, book reports, writing assignments (draft and final copies to show progress), reading log entries, poems, letters, and so forth as well as works in progress, with plans on how to finish/improve them

• Interview notes, journals, and other anecdotal records

• Audio or video tape recordings (readings, oral presentations, performances)

• Art work including pictures and graphs, charts, photos, story maps, and so on

• Tests and quizzes

• Checklists completed by students, peers, and teacher

♦ *How and when should items be selected?* Portfolios are a form of student–teacher partnership; and thus items may be teacher-selected, student-selected, or selected by both in conference. But because student participation in the selection process is critical, to reflect on their work and monitor their own progress, materials that are included should be *dated* and include an explanation for their inclusion, called a *reflection sheet* (otherwise, over time, students may forget why they included this item). Working on assembling a portfolio is a good anchor activity (students can do it whenever they finish something else and have a spare moment in class). Early in the school year, discussions with students need to teach them to ask the following:

- What would I like to reread or share with my parents or a friend?

- What makes a particular bit of class work a good product?

- What would show someone the best work I can do?

- What piece taught me something (an "aha!")?

- What shows I am making progress in something I had difficulty with?

- My students and I like to call these *VIP* (very important papers).

♦ *How and when should portfolios be evaluated?* Establish evaluation standards before the portfolio is begun. Portfolios are usually evaluated in terms of standards of excellence based on benchmarks or curriculum, or on growth demonstrated within an individual portfolio, rather than on comparisons made among different students' portfolios. Students' self-evaluation should explore areas needing more attention and effort as well as what they are now currently exploring and what their goals are for this class.

Good portfolios result from the following:

- Keeping the process simple

- Including more than just written work

- Asking students to explain and record (or reflect on) why they chose each work sample

- Maintaining a clear purpose

- Ensuring students have involvement and ownership

Nolen and Taylor in the book *Classroom Assessment* (2005) and Stiggins, Arter, Chappuis, and Chappuis in *Classroom Assessment for Student Learning* (2004) provide many good definitions and explanations of portfolios and their uses.

Pros and Cons of Using Portfolios

The following chart outlines the arguments for and against using portfolios.

Pro	Con
◆ Portfolios show students as individuals.	◆ Teachers must develop their own criteria, which can be initially time consuming, as well as possibly difficult or unfamiliar.
◆ Portfolios discourage teachers' comparison of students (rankings) and encourage evaluative feedback.	◆ Some parents and students might prefer standardized tests, considering portfolios to be more subjective and therefore less reliable or fair.
◆ They help teachers evaluate skills and knowledge without limiting creativity.	◆ Most colleges and universities still use test scores and grades for admissions, so portfolios would need to somehow translate into a grade.
◆ They make students more accountable for the work they do in class and the skills and knowledge we ask them to acquire.	◆ Portfolios are time consuming to use, requiring conferences and more extensive feedback, especially if portfolios are done in addition to traditional testing and grading.
◆ They ask students to engage in self-reflection on their growth and performance.	◆ Communication with students regarding portfolios and criteria for them must be very clear.
◆ Portfolios aid diversification, thus increasing the connections with a wider range of learners and learning styles.	
◆ They can involve parents and the community by helping them see their children's academic achievements and progress in the context of the school curriculum rather than as measured by standardized tests and grades.	

Subject Area Suggestions

Following are some suggestions from colleagues in various subject areas about using portfolios.

Portfolios for Language Arts

A language arts (or any other subject in which students write a lot) portfolio documents learning over time, and should show evidence of student improvement and self-assessment, editing, and revision. The following items go in a language arts portfolio:

- Table of contents: a written explanation of the contents of the portfolio as well as how it's organized
- Work assigned as benchmark assessments
- Free choice work: things students think are neat and want to share, as well as drafts, notes, finished and unfinished pieces.
- Reading/writing response logs or journals
- Student reflections on selected pieces
- Student organization plan
- Teacher notes
- Student notes: ideas for writing projects, editing ideas, notes about favorite authors or topics
- Letters and notes from others (parent notes, peer evaluations, etc.)
- Letters to/from authors
- Newspaper and magazine articles or pictures about favorite stories or authors
- Graphic organizers
- Videotapes of student performances
- Audiotapes of presentations
- Mind maps and notes
- Group reports
- Lists of books read
- Questionnaire results
- Tests and quizzes

Portfolios for Math

Items that could go in a math portfolio are as follows (based on National Council of Teachers of Mathematics standards for math portfolios http://www.ericdigests.org/2000–2/portfolio.htm):

♦ Table of contents

♦ Daily work: questions/problems

♦ Description about how students feel about math and/or an autobiography of their experiences with math

♦ Goal-setting sheets

♦ Standardized tests or information on such tests

♦ Journal entries

♦ Students' choice: individual or group work, analyses of problems, writing samples

♦ Projects, investigations

♦ Diagrams, graphs, photographs or pictures, reports

♦ Audio or video tapes of student/teacher interview or other events

♦ Evidence of the use of math in another discipline, or real-world applications

♦ Problems created by the student

Math Portfolio Grading Rubric

	Outstanding	**On Track**	**Emerging**	**Off Track**
General	♦ Exciting to look through ♦ Variety of written and graphic work ♦ Samples from beginning, middle, and end of term	♦ Variety of written work ♦ Work over time included	♦ Few projects, investigations, diagrams, etc. ♦ Work over time included	♦ Mostly worksheets, almost no creative work
Types of work	♦ Both individual and group work ♦ Evidence of use of multiple resources ♦ Extensive investigations of selected topics	♦ Some use of resources and group work ♦ Students obviously understand basic concepts	♦ Lack of work from all content areas, too much focus on one type	♦ See above
Thought processes evidenced	♦ Student analysis of information is shown ♦ Clear communication ♦ Self-assessment ♦ Enthusiasm	♦ Explains thought processes fairly well ♦ Self-assessment	♦ Minimal student explanation of process used ♦ Self-assessment	♦ No evidence of student discussion in class ♦ No explanation of thinking about math concepts

Adapted from Gresham, 1992, p. 19.

If you prefer a narrative rubric rather than the chart preceding, try something like this:

♦ Outstanding

In an outstanding portfolio, there is a theme or purpose, and everything included clearly indicates how and why it was chosen for the portfolio, and what learning or achievement it shows. Outsiders would easily understand and agree with the contents. A wide variety of articles are included, from various periods in the learning process. All curriculum standards are represented in the samples selected.

♦ On Track

An on-track portfolio shows student thought in selecting the piece and explaining the content, and there is evidence of student self-assessment. There are examples of most of the curriculum standards in the portfolio.

♦ Emerging

In an emerging portfolio there isn't enough information or organization for it to truly be a story of what learning has taken place. There is some evidence of reflection on the choices, but the student may not be able to explain the reasons clearly. Content of lessons is represented but not related to standards.

♦ Off Track

An off-track portfolio is simply a bunch of student work without an attempt on the part of the student to organize it, and minimal explanation that does little to clarify organization methods or explain learning.

Portfolios for Art

Art portfolios usually have three distinct sections:

1. *Quality*, the first, is usually works selected by the student that the student feels show a mastery of form, technique, and content.

2. *Concentration* illustrates investigation of method and/or style and self-assessment, as well as the process of discovery and growth.

3. *Breadth* permits the student to select works that demonstrate visual principles.

What to put into an art portfolio:

♦ Student work, which can be work done in class or on the student's own time

- Journal entries and reflective writing about art projects
- Peer reviews
- Self-assessments
- Student sketches, notes, photos, scans; and outlines, diagrams or charts
- Reports on art styles, artists, or other art-related topics
- Videotapes, audiotapes, or other forms of visual presentations

Portfolios for Science

Science portfolios are generally organized around units covered. A science portfolio generally contains, after a table of contents, the same types of items for each unit:

- Student unit summary
- Student work, generally an activity or experiment, data, any observations or drawings made, and a concluding statement
- A skills checklist for each piece, showing what process skills and critical thinking is involved in the activity
- Self-assessments

In addition, science portfolios may also contain the following:

- Journal entries and reflective writing about science
- Articles and news items about science
- Student sketches, notes, photos, scans, outlines, diagrams or charts
- Videotapes, audiotapes, or other forms of visual presentations
- Student investigations: surveys, suggestions of further experiments to conduct, etc.

A student reflection form to be used in portfolios is shown on the next page.

On pages 100–103 is a wonderful example of a portion of a four-part portfolio evaluation rubric from Shelly Barnes for use in a ninth-grade class. I like that it provides for higher-level thinking skills as well as peer evaluations. It would require, I think, a large commitment of time to use as an evaluation instrument.

(Text continues on page 106.)

Student Reflection Form

Page: _____

Name:_____   Date: _____

Title or topic of item: _____

Description of item: _____

_____

_____

(Continue on back if necessary)

Why do you feel this represents high-quality work?

What are the three most important ideas or skills* you learned from doing this entry? (Don't just list them; explain briefly!)

Where could you improve, change, or strengthen this item?

What suggestions would you have for another student wanting to do something like this?

Signatures: Advisor: _____

                     Advisee: _____

*SKILLS LIST

♦ Acquiring and processing information through independent learning

♦ Applying science knowledge to real-world situations

♦ Communicating in graphic or oral or written form

♦ Improving work through peer and self-evaluation

♦ Using decision-making/problem-solving skills

♦ Using the inquiry process to plan and carry out an investigation

♦ Working collaboratively

Group Project Guidelines

(Thanks to Shelley Barnes)

Objectives	Low Performance (5 Points)	At or Below Average (10 Points)	At or Above Average (15 Points)	Exemplary Performance (20 Points)	Earned Points	Peer Evaluation
Project demonstrates familiarity with the subject (20)	Project shows familiarity with main ideas and details relating to one of the following: obesity, healthy eating plan, food guide pyramid, exercise	Project shows familiarity with main ideas and details relating to two of the following: obesity, healthy eating plan, food guide pyramid, exercise	Project shows familiarity with main ideas and details relating to three of the following: obesity, healthy eating plan, food guide pyramid, exercise	Project shows familiarity with main ideas and details relating to all of the following: obesity, healthy eating plan, food guide pyramid, exercise		
Layout and Design (20)	Beginning attempts to combine organization, design, use of color and use of space to make the project interesting and communicate the message	Developing ways to combine organization, design, use of color, and use of space to make the project interesting and communicate the message	Satisfactory work that combines organization, design, use of color, and use of space to make the project interesting and communicate the message	Exemplary work that combines organization, design, use of color, and use of space to make the project interesting and communicate the message		

Mechanics (CUP) (20)	There are several errors in capitalization, usage, punctuation, or spelling	There are some errors in capitalization, usage, punctuation, or spelling	There are very few errors in capitalization, usage, punctuation, or spelling	There are no errors in capitalization, usage, punctuation, or spelling	
Group Work (20)	Group could not complete assignment	Only one person worked to complete the project	Everyone in the group worked together to complete the assignment	Everyone worked in the group to go above and beyond the requirements of the project	
Timeliness (20)	Project turned in a week late or more	Project turned in 3 days late	Project turned in 2 days late	Project turned in on time	

Score Earned

Peer Comments	
Teacher Comments	

Student Portfolio Rubric

Objectives	Low Performance (5 Points)	At or Below Average (10 Points)	At or Above Average (15 Points)	Exemplary Performance (20 Points)	Earned Points	Peer Evaluation
Project demonstrates familiarity with the subject (20)	Project shows familiarity with main ideas and details relating to one of the following: obesity, healthy eating plan, food guide pyramid, exercise	Project shows familiarity with main ideas and details relating to two of the following: obesity, healthy eating plan, food guide pyramid, exercise	Project shows familiarity with main ideas and details relating to three of the following: obesity, healthy eating plan, food guide pyramid, exercise	Project shows familiarity with main ideas and details relating to all of the following: obesity, healthy eating plan, food guide pyramid, exercise		
Layout and Design (20)	Beginning attempts to combine organization, design, use of color and use of space to make the project interesting and communicate the message	Developing ways to combine organization, design, use of color, and use of space to make the project interesting and communicate the message	Satisfactory work that combines organization, design, use of color, and use of space to make the project interesting and communicate the message	Exemplary work that combines organization, design, use of color, and use of space to make the project interesting and communicate the message		

Mechanics (CUP) (20)	There are several errors in capitalization, punctuation, usage, or spelling	There are some errors in capitalization, usage, punctuation, or spelling	There are very few errors in capitalization, usage, punctuation, or spelling	There are no errors in capitalization, usage, punctuation, or spelling
Group Work (20)	Group could not complete assignment	Only one person worked to complete the project	Everyone in the group worked together to complete the assignment	Everyone worked in the group to go above and beyond the requirements of the project
Timeliness (20)	Project turned in a week late or more	Project turned in 3 days late	Project turned in 2 days late	Project turned in on time

Score Earned

Peer Comments

Teacher Comments

Types of Assessment for Portfolios

Portfolios are not something you assess only once. There are several levels of assessment:

Advisory assessment is when you check over the portfolio to see how it's progressing, and advise students on what is still needed as well as their success in time management (or lack of it). You would also check for self-assessment and reflection pieces for each item.

A *conference* is a one-on-one meeting with the student when you sit down and go over what the student thinks is a finished portfolio. This is when you can assign a grade (if desired) or you could consider this like the dress rehearsal for a play.

In the *exhibition phase*, the student presents the portfolio to an audience. The audience could be parents and relatives, a panel of faculty members, a group of classmates or students from a more advanced class in the same subject, some school administrators, or another group such as science fair judges or community members (as in an art show). The audience could ask questions, provide feedback, and/or evaluate the portfolio.

Projects

There are basically two ways to have students do projects: as a final unit assessment (or even a semester test), and by student choice.

Teacher-Assigned Projects

As a believer in alternative methods of assessment, I have designed quite a few final projects for my students that demonstrate everything in the unit and have taken the place of a book-generated test. For example, for a unit on the imperfect versus the *passé composé* (Spanish: preterit), every one in the class selects a different (famous) painting from a folder I've assembled (old calendars, cut apart). They are told that they were also there, with those people, looking at the same scene. They must describe that day as a fond or scary or important memory: who was there, where they were, weather, clothing, who was doing what, and so forth. Then suddenly (they must use the word *soudain*) something new happened. They are to tell what happened immediately after the moment shown in the painting. I get some wonderful flights of fancy, practicing dictionary and diction skills, as well as the two past tenses. These students have choices of content, but not of product.

This is an example of a teacher-assigned project that allows students to demonstrate competencies and knowledge based on input of their own choice but with an end result that will, at least superficially, all resemble each other in form (but not in content).

Student Choice Project

The other type of project may not be assigned to an entire class but to select groups. You may remember that in compacting, students may select an activity to do while others do more traditional unit study. A project is one of their choices. Students who have a strong interest in a particular subject may wish to work with you, or a community mentor, to design an independent study of their interest area.

The most important element of any project is *engageability*. To have a successful project, you need to arrange the following for each student:

♦ To be engrossed in learning something somewhat challenging

♦ To be involved in a real-world task or application

♦ To learn by doing

♦ To be able to effectively diagnose where she or he is and what to do next

♦ To communicate his or her learning

The second most important element is a good checklist or rubric, so students are aware of what is required and can self-assess their success while completing the project (see Chapter 7 for more on rubrics, or Appendix 3 for checklists).

The third element is the student's comfort level. I'd like to advocate making the project choices correlate with Gardner's learning styles (see the end of this chapter for subject-specific suggestions or Appendix 1 for a general list of choices).

In each unit, you should plan at least one such activity. This procedure allows each student to choose and create a product that plays to his or her strengths, increasing the student's comfort level as to whether he or she will be successful in completing the project. For example, in a history class, while learning causes of the Civil War, one student might write a song, another might create a piece of dialogue between two historical characters, and a third might write a piece of illustrated historical fiction such as a letter from a soldier, a freed slave, or a sweetheart left behind (like in the movie *Cold Mountain*).

A fourth element is authenticity. Connecting the world of school with a student's own experiences or interests makes the project more relevant, more equitable and more enjoyable for everyone. To achieve this element, you need to involve the students in helping plan the project.

The final, most important element is a good checklist. Project checklists not only help learners target the desired skills, but also use metacognition (self-assessment); allow students to chart progress toward completion; and, for slower students, break the assignment down into small, manageable parts. And the students basically know, before they ever hand in the project, what grade it will receive, because they know the degree of completion they've achieved according to the checklist. Appendix 3 is a variety of checklists to look at as a starting point for creating your own.

I know lots of people use rubrics, but those take much, much longer to write, longer to use in evaluation, and are harder for students to use to self-evaluate, as well (especially if they have poor reading skills or a short attention span).

These checklists could also be used by a classmate to do a peer review before it is handed in. I like to have it peer-checked for several reasons. First, students need to have the project done a bit in advance of deadline to have time to have someone else look it over. Second, students might hand in something junky if it was for my eyes only, but they take more care if a classmate will see it. Third, there is always a chance that the classmate, when reading another project, will see in it things that he or she could improve in his or her own project. And finally, the fewer errors in a product, the faster the grading process goes for me!

Sample Projects

I am happy to include here two sets of projects used in social studies classes. The first is the creative combination of student interest in baseball or other types of trading cards with some research into famous people and is supplied by Nina Kendall of Eagle's Landing High School in McDonough, Georgia.

Greek and Roman Trading Cards Activity

♦ Assessment for Learning

This assessment is designed to help students learn about the contributions that the Greeks and Romans made to the development of their society and to Western civilization as a whole.

♦ Activity

This activity should be assigned to students at the beginning of a unit on Greek and Roman Civilizations. It has two phases: (a) the research of important figures in Greece and Rome and (b) the activity of creating trading cards. Students should be assessed for participation in both phases of the activity. The task cards are provided so that students can be assigned a version of this lesson that best suits their current classroom performance and learning style.

♦ Product Descriptors

Rubric, sample trading card, notes sheet (p. 108), task cards (pp. 109–110), sample student assignment with rubric (pp. 111–112).

◆ Selecting the Task

The task assigned to the students should be the one that best suits their ability to achieve success in the classroom. If you want to give students a choice, the students should be offered a choice of two of the tasks: one they can accomplish with success and one that offers them an academic challenge.

◆ Procedures

1. Students should be provided with rubric, sample trading card, and note-taking sheet at the opening of the unit.

2. Discuss the importance of selecting appropriate and valid information.

3. Inform students that the note-taking sheet should be completed at the midpoint of the unit.

4. Students may be allowed to work on the sheet in class as they read and for homework. (*I check the work for completion and review the importance of each figure as the lesson progresses.*)

5. The cards should be due 2 to 3 days before the final assessment for the unit. (*Students may ask for feedback on their cards and notes prior to completion. The cards were completed largely at home, but students could work on them in class.*)

6. Students should be encouraged to develop their own ranking system for their cards. You can use the examples of grading movies or 5-star service to explain the concept.

◆ Evaluation

The rubric addresses both the *content* and *construction* of their cards. It does not address the quality of their note taking sheet, which is assessed for completion. The opportunity for oral defense is provided so that students may defend the validity of one or more choices they made in selecting content for their cards, and ranking them. The rubric should be reviewed with the students in detail when the activity is assigned, and students will be able to self-assess their project by using the same rubric.

Some more options for the social studies project might be the following:

◆ Describe how today's world might be different without that person's contributions.

◆ Predict what that famous person might be doing today if he were alive right now

(*Text continues on page 113.*)

Trading Cards Note-Taking Sheet

Famous Greeks

Name	Achievements and Contributions to Civilization
Plato	
Socrates	
Aristotle	
Alexander the Great	
Homer	

Famous Romans

Name	Achievements and Contributions to Civilization
Hannibal	
Julius Caesar	
Augustus	
Virgil	
Marcus Aurelius	

Trading Card
Rubrics and Sample Card

Trading Card Rubric						
Requirements	Excellent	Good	Fair	Poor	None	Total
Quality of Content	48	36	24	12	0	
Image	16	12	8	4	0	
Minimum of 5 facts	12	9	6	3	0	
Format of Card	12	9	6	3	0	
Spelling and Punctuation	12	9	6	3	0	
					Grade	

Oral Defense Rubric	
Score	Performance Description
4	The response shows a thorough understanding of the topic and extends on the information provided in the activity. The response is logical and well thought out.
3	The response demonstrators knowledge of the topic but does not discuss the importance of the topic. The response shows limited understanding of the topic in the context of the subject studied.
2	The response demonstrates little understanding of the topic or its importance. The response is based on limited information about the topic and does not include a reasoned defense.
1	The response demonstrates little or no knowledge of the topic and is characterized by misunderstandings.

(Figure continues on next page.)

Bald Eagle

Endangered Species Trading Cards

Facts About the Bald Eagle

♦ The Bald Eagle is a national symbol for the United States.

♦ It is on the U.S. Endangered Species List.

♦ The Bald Eagle is classified as threatened in all the contiguous United States.

♦ The biggest threat to the Bald Eagle continues to be poisoning from pesticides and other chemicals that pollute the environment.

♦ You can help ensure the Bald Eagle survives by limiting your use of toxic chemicals and disposing of them properly so they don't pollute the environment.

Rank: 5 Out of 5 Hearts

♥ ♥ ♥ ♥ ♥

Endangered Species

Most Valuable Species

The Bald Eagle earns top recognition as the "Most Valuable Species" in this series of trading cards in recognition of the success of the bald eagle conservation effort. The bald eagle population has shown record growth in the last 20 years. The success rate of this conservation program makes it a model of success for other conservation efforts to emulate.

Sample Greek and Roman
Trading Card Activity Task Cards

Greek and Roman Trading Card Activity A	
Trading Card Task	Create a set of Famous Greeks and Romans Trading Cards that describe the significant achievements and contributions of famous people from the past. Rate each person's contribution to the development of Greek or Roman Civilization. Select an MVP (Most Valuable Person) for both civilizations and justify your choice for MVP.

Requirements	◆ 8 cards in your set featuring an equal number of Greeks and Romans
	
	◆ Image for each card
	
	◆ List:
	  • Title or profession (Examples: emperor, author, scientist)
	  • 3 nouns or adjectives that describe the person
	  • 1 important accomplishment
	
	◆ Rating indicating importance of person to the development of that civilization (e.g., 4 out 5 stars)
	
	◆ MVP for both civilizations with justification for their recognition

Greek and Roman Trading Card Activity B	
Trading Card Task	Create a set of Famous Greeks and Romans Trading Cards that describe the significant achievements and contributions of famous people from the past. Rate each person's contribution to the development of Greek or Roman Civilization. Select an MVP (Most Valuable Person) for both civilizations and justify your choice for MVP.
Requirements	◆ 8 cards in your set featuring an equal number of Greeks and Romans. ◆ Image for each card. ◆ Your card should include 5 facts that express the importance of the subject of the card to the development of Greek or Roman Civilization. ◆ Rating indicating importance of person to the development of that civilization (e.g., 4 out 5 stars). ◆ MVP for both civilizations with justification for their recognition.

(Figure continues on next page.)

Greek and Roman Trading Card Activity C	
Trading Card Task	Create a set of Famous Greeks and Romans Trading Cards that describe the significant achievements and contributions of famous people from the past. Rate each person's contribution to the development of Greek or Roman Civilization. Select an MVP (Most Valuable Person) for both civilizations and justify your choice for MVP.
Requirements	◆ 8 cards in your set featuring an equal number of Greeks and Romans. ◆ Image for each card and a personal symbol for the subject of the card that represents their legacy to modern civilization. ◆ Your card should include a well-written paragraph that discusses the contribution the subject of the card made to the development of Greek or Roman Civilization. ◆ Rating indicating importance of person to the development of that civilization (e.g., 4 out 5 stars). ◆ MVP for both civilizations with justification for their recognition.

Enrichment Projects

This second project is supplied by Marcia Losco, social studies teacher at Yorktown Middle School in Yorktown, Indiana. She says, "The Enrichment Projects assignment sheet I sent is for eighth grade social studies, which is U.S. history from the American Revolution to 1877. I use the project choices with any unit, but sometimes I have different requirements on presentation of the projects. I used it most recently on our Civil War research project."

- ◆ Write an acrostic poem:
  - Research your topic and take notes to gather 50 facts.
  - Record facts on note-taking forms.
  - Include at least *two* facts in each line of the acrostic poem.
  - Use color to make topic title more visible in the poem.
  - Include five appropriate illustrations.
  - Turn in notes and poem.

- ◆ Make an oral report to the class:
  - Research your topic and take notes to gather 50 facts.
  - Record facts on note-taking forms.
  - Prepare note cards to use during your oral presentation.
  - Your oral presentation must last at least *three* minutes.
  - Create a *colorful* visual aid to supplement your oral presentation.
  - Turn in note-taking forms, *note cards,* and visual aid.

- ◆ Write a piece of historical fiction:
  - Research your topic and take notes to gather 50 facts.
  - Record facts on note-taking forms.
  - Combine facts with your imagination to create a series of letters, journal entries, or a story that includes the facts from your research.
  - Create a colorful and historically appropriate cover page.
  - Turn in your notes with a final copy of your fiction piece.

- ◆ Create a newspaper reporting historical events:
  - Research several topics and gather a total of 50 facts.
  - Record facts on note-taking forms.
  - Choose a location and a name for your newspaper and create an attractive flag for the top of the paper.

- Using the facts gathered, create at least one newspaper article about each topic.

- Display articles in a newspaper format with columns, headlines, bylines, and datelines for each article.

- Turn in notes and newspaper.

♦ Gather statistics and present your findings in a graph(s):

- Research your topic to gather 50 facts.

- Record facts on note-taking forms.

- Title the graph(s) to explain the content.

- Label the graph appropriately.

- Use color to make the graph(s) easy to read.

- Turn in the graph(s) and your notes.

♦ Compare two topics using a Venn diagram:

- Research each topic to gather at least 25 facts on each.

- Record the facts on note-taking forms.

- Group the facts according to similarities and differences.

- Display a total of 25 facts in the appropriate places on the Venn diagram.

- Use color to make the diagram interesting and attractive.

- Add at least one illustration for each topic researched.

- Turn in notes and Venn diagram.

♦ Create an illustrated timeline poster:

- Research your topic to gather 50 facts.

- Record facts on note-taking forms.

- Choose 15 events to place on a timeline.

- Create a timeline that is clearly labeled with dates and marked in even increments to serve as a baseline.

- Insert your chosen events in the appropriate places along the timeline.

- Label each event with a title, a date, and its significance.

- Use the facts gathered to help you create an appropriate illustration for each event to make the timeline interesting.

- Use color to make the timeline attractive.

- Turn in your notes and the timeline.

- ◆ Create a map to illustrate a topic in history:
  - Research a topic to gather at least 50 facts.
  - Record facts on note-taking forms.
  - Create a historically accurate map to illustrate facts researched.
  - Use color to make the map attractive.
  - Add at least *five* illustrations to the map.
  - Turn in notes and map.
- ◆ Create a model, sample, or diorama of an artifact:
  - Research a topic to gather at least 50 facts.
  - Record facts on note-taking forms.
  - Use the facts gathered to create a realistic model.
  - Label the model to explain parts, materials, purposes, steps in construction, and so forth.
  - Use color to make the model look realistic.
  - Turn in notes along with model.
- ◆ Write a song with lyrics that explain a historical topic:
  - Research a topic and gather at least 50 facts.
  - Record facts on note-taking forms.
  - Use the facts gathered to create lyrics for a song.
  - Compose your own music or use the melody from a popular song you know.
  - Perform or record the lyrics and the melody.
  - Turn in notes and lyrics or a recording.
- ◆ Create a picture display:
  - Research your topic to gather at least 50 facts.
  - Record facts on note-taking forms.
  - Gather at least 15 photographs or pictures related to your topic.
  - Create a display that includes the following:
    - Pictures with a caption for each
    - Sources of the pictures
    - Color to make display attractive and interesting
  - Turn in notes and picture display.
- ◆ Create a poster of historical heads:

- Research an individual to gather at least 25 facts.

- Record facts on note-taking forms.

- Create a poster in the shape of a profile of a human head.

- Use the person's name as the title, and fill the head with at least 5 images to represent ideas, thoughts, visions, motivations, and so forth of the famous person. Number each image.

- On the back of the poster, include a numbered key with a statement explaining how each image on the front relates to the person.

- Use color to make poster attractive.

- Turn in notes with head profile.

♦ Create bumper stickers:

- Research a topic to gather at least 25 facts.

- Record facts on note-taking forms.

- On 11×4-inch paper, create a bumper sticker with a catchy slogan that is historically appropriate and includes facts from research.

- Use color and illustrations to make sticker interesting and attractive.

- Turn in notes with bumper sticker

Neatness, spelling, grammar, and following directions are always part of your grade.

Civil War Research Projects

Working in English and social studies classes, students will research a Civil War topic.

The requirements for social studies class are as follows:

♦ Research your assigned topic to gather 70 facts on note cards.

♦ Note cards must be submitted to _____ for a fact check on _____.

♦ Working outside of class, students create a project based on their research. Your choices are listed below.

♦ All projects will be shared with the class in a history fair presentation.

♦ Class presentations must include a neatly prepared copy of the preliminary outline (in ink) with each question clearly answered in complete sentences.

♦ Below the preliminary outline answers, students must list 10 additional facts gathered through research.

♦ At the time of the presentation, a table sign must be displayed with a one-sentence summary of the importance of your topic for the Civil War.

- ◆ Write an acrostic poem:
  - Research your topic and take notes to gather 70 facts.
  - Record facts on note cards.
  - Using the complete title, include at least *two* facts in each line of the acrostic poem.
  - Use color to make topic title more visible in the poem.
  - Include 5 appropriate illustrations.
- ◆ Make an oral report to the class:
  - Research your topic and take notes to gather 70 facts.
  - Record facts on note cards.
  - Prepare additional note cards to use during your oral presentation.
  - Your oral presentation must last at least *3* minutes.
  - Create a *colorful* visual aid with a title and at least five visuals to supplement your oral presentation.
- ◆ Write a piece of historical fiction:
  - Research your topic and take notes to gather 70 facts.
  - Record facts on note cards.
  - Combine facts with your imagination to create a series of letters, journal entries, or a story that includes at least 25 facts from your research.
  - Highlight the facts where they appear in the text of your fiction.
  - Create a colorful and historically appropriate cover page.
- ◆ Create a newspaper reporting historical events:
  - Research to gather a total of 70 facts.
  - Record facts on note cards.
  - Choose a location and a name for your newspaper and create an attractive flag with a Civil War theme for the top of the paper.
  - Using the facts gathered, separate your research into at least three topics and create at least one newspaper article about each topic.
  - Display articles in a newspaper format with columns, headlines, bylines, and datelines for each article.
- ◆ Gather statistics and present your findings in a series of graphs:
  - Research your topic to gather 70 facts.
  - Record facts on note cards.
  - Title the graphs to explain the content and include 25 facts.

- Label the graphs appropriately with keys and explanations.
- Use color to make the graphs easy to read and add at least three pictures.

◆ Create a Venn diagram:

- Research to gather 70 facts.
- Record the facts on note cards.
- Group the facts according to similarities and differences.
- Display a total of 25 facts in the appropriate places on a Venn diagram.
- Use color to make the diagram interesting and attractive.
- Add at least two illustrations for each section of the Venn.

◆ Create an illustrated timeline poster:

- Research your topic to gather 70 facts.
- Record facts on note cards.
- Choose 15 events to place on a timeline that is clearly labeled with dates and marked in even increments to serve as a baseline.
- Insert your chosen events in the appropriate places along the timeline.
- Label each event with a title, a date, and its significance.
- Create an appropriate illustration for each event.
- Use color to make the timeline attractive.

◆ Create a map to illustrate a topic in history:

- Research a topic to gather at least 70 facts.
- Record facts on note cards.
- Create a historically accurate map to illustrate facts researched.
- Label the map with facts and include a key.
- Use color to make the map attractive.
- Add at least five illustrations to the map.

◆ Create a model, sample, or diorama of an artifact:

- Research a topic to gather at least 70 facts.
- Record facts on note cards.
- Use the facts gathered to create a realistic model.
- Label the model to explain parts, materials, purposes, steps in construction, events in series, and so forth.
- Use color to make the model look realistic.

♦ Write a song with lyrics that explain a historical topic:

  • Research a topic and gather at least 70 facts.

  • Record facts on note cards.

  • Use 25 of the facts gathered to create lyrics for a song.

  • Compose your own music or use the melody from a popular song you know.

  • Display the lyrics on a poster with at least five appropriate visuals.

  • Highlight the facts on the poster.

  • Perform or record the lyrics and the melody.

♦ Create a picture display:

  • Research your topic to gather at least 70 facts.

  • Record facts on note cards.

  • Gather at least 15 photographs/pictures related to your topic.

  • Display the pictures with a caption for each that includes at least two facts.

  • Use color to make display attractive and interesting.

All pictures included in projects must have their sources cited. Effort (including neatness, spelling, grammar, and following directions) is always part of your grade.

Health Project

A third project, contributed by Shelly Barnes, a physical education teacher, allows for a wide variety of student choice, and clearly spells out how the project will proceed and be assessed.

To complete your project the following things need to be included to what you have already done:

♦ Fitness Contract, Fitness Plan, overall reflection on did your fitness level improve or not (explain why you think it did or didn't), what do you plan to do to stay *Fit for Life*?

♦ You need to make sure every slide from the beginning to the end has a personal tie back to you. I'm not looking for generic information; I'm looking for information that relates to you.

♦ Make sure there are no grammatical errors—PROOFREAD!!

♦ Include pictures of you!!! This is a project about you!

♦ Fix errors and consider suggestions I have given you.

I. Fitness Contract:

♦ Start date

♦ Need to design a contract in paragraph or outline form that states how you plan to implement your fitness plan.

♦ This probably should be done after you design your Fitness Plan to stay healthy for life.

♦ State goals, rewards, and so forth.

II. Fitness Plan:

♦ Set realistic goals and list them out (short-term goals and long-term goals).

♦ What steps will you take to reach your goals (be specific)? Think about nutrition, exercise, and so forth.

♦ Identify potential problems and ways to get help and support from others.

♦ Set up check points to evaluate your progress.

♦ What will be your rewards to yourself for meeting your goals?

Basics of designing a Physical Activity Plan:

♦ Overload: working the body harder than it is normally worked

♦ Progression: gradual increase in overload necessary to achieve higher levels of fitness

♦ Specificity: particular exercises and activities improve particular areas of health-related fitness

Example of How to Start a Physical Activity Plan

You need to identify the following for your plan:

Who	What	When	Where	Why
Alone, with a partner, team, family, and so forth.	Variety of activities you will enjoy and do, and at what intensity level? What are my goals?	How often, how long?	Fitness center, at home, friends house, walk at track, and so forth.	Why are you choosing this particular exercise? What elements of fitness are you using?

Library dates:_____

Due date for entire project:_____

Suggestions by Subject Area

Here is another long list of other possibilities, by subject area (but you might just want to read other areas for ideas, as well), for Gardner's eight intelligences:

History

- Argue different sides' perspectives from a war or conflict.
- Compare or contrast different periods of history.
- Create a history rap using key dates.
- Create analogies between historical events and natural events.
- Create time sequence charts for major eras of history.
- Debate important issues and decisions from the past.
- Discuss the impact of key historical decisions on today's world.
- Do a plus and minus analysis chart of famous historical decisions.
- Find examples of history repeating itself.
- Have a historical costumes and food day.
- Have an imaginary interview or talk with people from the past.
- Imagine people from the past giving you advice today: What would they say?
- Imagine you are participating in a historical event: What do you see/hear/smell/touch/feel/think/believe?
- *Jigsaw* an historical period (groups of students each learn part and teach it to others).
- Make visuals (diagrams, flow charts) of historical events.
- Paint a mural about a period of history.
- Play charades with historical events.
- Play *What's My Line?* with historical figures.
- Predict what the next decade will be like, based on patterns from the past.
- Reenact moments or scenes from history.
- Reflect: If I could be any person in history, who would I be, and why?
- Study poetry/literature/music/dances from different periods in history.

- Understand how natural events such as weather have influenced history.

- Write an imaginary conversation/interview with a famous person.

Geography and global studies

- Create a scenario for *culture shock* and analyze its causes.

- Describe your ideal geography and climate, and find at least one place on a map where both exist.

- Discuss how you'd be different if you had grown up in a different culture.

- Discuss ways to overcome the *ugly American* stereotype, and prioritize steps to take.

- Draw a map from memory, and compare it to a real map.

- From the perspective of a different culture, comment on a current news item.

- Invent a new country. Describe its geography and culture. Draw a map of it.

- Learn, taste, and grow foods from different cultures.

- Learn basic phrases in the language of another culture.

- Learn folk dances/songs from another culture.

- Look at a road map and give verbal instructions to get somewhere on the map.

- Make a map in clay, showing geographical features.

- Make decorations for the classroom about a culture being studied.

- Play games from another culture.

- Predict what will happen in several current-event stories.

- Read and learn stories, myths, and poetry from other cultures.

- Simulate a shopping trip in another country (using their currency).

- Study the visual art of a culture.

- Study the effect of climate/geography on cultural development.

- Teach someone else how to read different kinds of maps.

- Use a map to locate sites in an unfamiliar location.

English/Language Arts

- Act out a portion of a story or play being read, without words, and have others guess what part you are doing.

- Create songs/raps to teach grammar, syntax, phonetics, semantics or other concepts.

- Draw a storyboard for a story, book or play being read.

- Find and analyze elements in a story that apply to your own life.

- Give an impromptu speech.

- Imagine being a character in literature: What would you do differently or the same?

- Read a book with a partner, and write messages/journal entries back and forth between you about what you are reading.

- Use a story grid or other graphic organizer for creative writing activities.

- Use *concept mapping* to remember and organize content.

- Use highlighter markers to color a story or poem, and explain what method was used for deciding what color each portion should be.

- Write a piece (essay, poem, story) based on a musical work.

- Write a sequel/next episode to a story or play.

- Write a story from the perspective of an animal or a plant.

Mathematics

- Conduct a survey/research project and calculate and show the results.

- Create number sequences and have others try to find the patterns.

- Design classification charts for math formulas, processes and operations.

- Evaluate your strengths/weaknesses in understanding math and plan new strategies for success.

- Find and show mathematical patterns in the natural world and environment.

- Graph positive and negative influences on the environment.

- Have your team construct problems linking many math operations, and then solve them (and have other teams solve it).

- Invent something that requires applying math concepts.

- Learn metric measurements and apply them to daily life situations.

- Make up a playground-style game that uses math concepts/operations.

- Make up sounds and gestures for different math operations and processes.
- Mind-map proofs for geometric theorems.
- Teach a group to solve complex story problems.
- Use different body parts as a *ruler* to measure things.

Science and Health

- Act out different states of matter.
- Create a collage on a science topic.
- Create an experiment, writing the steps so someone else can perform it easily.
- Describe the before and the after of key scientific paradigm shifts.
- Devise five different ways to classify a group of similar objects (e.g., leaf collection).
- Discuss and create ways to say no to drugs.
- Draw and label the pattern of successful and reliable scientific experiments.
- Give a speech on *Ten Ways to Healthful Living*.
- Illustrate different parts of a healthy diet.
- Keep a diary of the natural processes of your own body.
- Make up an imaginary conversation between different parts of the body or parts of a cell.
- Pretend you are microscopic, and describe a trip you take.
- Role play the parts (and dynamics) of a plant or animal cell.
- Role play the rotation of planets in the solar system.
- Study and try various biofeedback techniques/methods.
- Use symbols from the periodic table of the elements in a story.
- Web (graphic) the various systems of the body.
- Write a diary from the perspective of a red or white blood cell.
- Write a humorous story or poem using science vocabulary or formulas.
- Write a position paper (or have a panel discussion) on a controversial health topic.

NOTE: This site has fully supported, standards-based, community-connected science projects: http://www.k12science.org/collabprojs.html/.

Practical Arts/Physical Education

♦ Create a Jeopardy-style game for this unit.

♦ Create a new food, article of clothing, game/sport, or machine: Make it and explain it, as well as teach others to use/eat/perform it.

♦ Create instructions (including visual) for using a certain machine or appliance.

♦ Experiment with the effects of different kinds of music on performance.

♦ Find someone who uses skills in this unit in real life; interview or write a report on this.

♦ Grow something and use it in cooking.

♦ Imagine a computer (or other machine) is human, and draw (or explain) how it works.

♦ Journal everything done when producing a product or performing a specific task: activities, thoughts, and feelings as you do this, physical responses, and so forth.

♦ Learn about natural materials used in construction and manufacturing.

♦ Learn how to use nature responsibly and appropriately in industrial technology.

♦ Prepare and serve meals from foreign countries, or using unusual ingredients.

♦ Understand the good and bad points of different fabrics based on their natural content.

♦ Work with a partner to improve cooking/sports/technology skills (plan for and track participation and improvement).

♦ Write a problem-solving scenario for this unit/subject.

Fine Arts

♦ Create an interpretive dance based on a piece of music, poem, event, mood, machine or the like.

♦ Create/draw sets for various scenes of a play or dance.

♦ Create using something from nature/the environment (sounds, objects, movements).

- Learn a new skill (art, music, dance, etc.) and teach it to others (team product).

- Make up a story about an art object, piece of music, etc.

- Recognize and recreate patterns and/or images from nature.

- Turn a nonmusical play, short story or poem into a musical one.

- Turn a serious play into a comedy, or vice versa.

- Write a play or piece of music.

NOTE: This site contains lots of useful tools for music students: www.apple.com/support/garageband/. Why not ask them to become an expert on one, and share with the class? Last of all there's a free toolbox-type resource for teachers (after joining, also free) to help create projects at http://www.pbl-online.org/.

Summary

A good summative assessment enables students to show their level of knowledge of a subject. A good *differentiated* summative assessment allows students to design and control the style of assessment according to their interests, preferred performance style, and comfort level, to show a degree of creativity, and to self-evaluate throughout the assessment process. Compacting allows them to accelerate when they feel capable, projects involve them in higher-level thinking, and portfolios make them reflective learners. Students not only perceive this as more fair, but also as more interesting and motivating.

6

Use Technology in Assessment

Technology in schools is a rapidly increasing educational resource, and there is some pressure to use it as much as possible. As technological forms of assessment are growing in popularity and more available, it is used increasingly as well; and at the printing of this book, cell phones, podcasts, and i-movies are the latest frontiers to explore for use as assessment options.

Technology-based assessment, just as all the other forms already discussed here, can be

- ♦ diagnostic (to assess level of competence),

- ♦ self-assessing (for students to check their own understanding of material),

- ♦ formative (to give students feedback), and

- ♦ summative (end of unit evaluation).

The essential idea to keep in mind is whether using technology would benefit students more than a more traditional pencil-and-paper activity. Will this use of technology enable students to do something that they could not do before, or do something now that they could do before but can do better now?

Benefits of Using Computer Assessment

Technology is *worth it* in the following cases:

- ♦ It fits a curricular goal (of course!).

- ♦ Students get immediate feedback on their performance. *Tutorial support* explains to them why an incorrect answer is incorrect, and even gives them more practice on that skill in some cases.

- ♦ Students are motivated to get involved and to work harder and for longer periods of time.

- Multiple delivery modes are possible (audio, visual, textual) to appeal to different learning styles, and especially to adapt to the needs of special needs students. A *read aloud* feature benefits students with visual recognition deficits like dyslexia or poor vision; the use of colorful graphics and other features such as timelines appeal to many.

- It provides a real audience with a real interest in what's written, such as a link to a web publishing site or an online project (especially useful in compacting or spin-off situations).

- Critical thinking skills are practiced, such as comparing similarities and differences, analysis of data found, discussion, or distinguishing fact from opinion.

- Students using it engage in more self-reflective and constructive criticism.

- Students using it experience success.

Four Focuses of Technology

Inquiry	Communication	Construction	Expression
◆ Spreadsheets	◆ Word processing	◆ Robotics	◆ Interactive video
◆ Online databases	◆ Graphics software	◆ Computer-aided design	◆ Animation software
◆ Hypertext	◆ Tutorials	◆ Control systems	◆ Music composition
◆ Online observatories, such as microscopes	◆ Conferencing, blogs, and chats	◆ Online projects	◆ Podcasts
	◆ Simulations		◆ Blogs
	◆ E-mail		◆ Chats

The *inquiry* type of technology is less applicable to assessment (however, one could ask students to construct something using that technology) but the other forms could all be used easily as assessments.

Using technology is another way to customize and adapt assessment, as well as allow for a more interactive form of assessment. Today there are computer programs that not only help students; but in tracking student success, they give more information about how the student is learning. For example, I have used a writing program that, at first, just asked questions to be answered in essay form, but which now has built-in spelling help and which can read aloud what was written and allow for voice recognition entry of text (great for partially sighted or blind students) and the insertion of media such as videos, graphics and sounds to enhance the narrative. You can also add prompts to help students self-monitor and edit. The teacher can also access information on what supports a student used, the strategies he or she followed (and which they seem to have missed), and gain insight into what the student has or has not grasped about the writing process.

Computerized Adaptive Testing*

In computerized adaptive testing (CAT), the computer administering the test actually individually *tailors* the test to the student's achievement level. Generally, the first question is of middle-level difficulty; and if the student, using a keyboard or computer mouse, answers incorrectly, it offers somewhat easier questions. If the student correctly answers the question, a slightly more difficult question is offered. The principal result of this is that the number of questions required to reach a pass or fail decision is considerably fewer and thus the test time is shorter, a motivating factor especially for students with disabilities. Other advantages of CAT include the following:

♦ *Graduated difficulty.* Students are offered questions at their ability level and are not frustrated by too-difficult or annoyed by too-easy items.

♦ *Immediate feedback.* The test can be scored immediately, providing instantaneous feedback.

♦ *Improved test security.* The computer program contains a large pool of questions, rather than the handful that make up any individual's test. As a result, it is more difficult to artificially boost one's scores by merely learning a few items or even types of items.

♦ *Possibility of multimedia format.* Tests can include text, graphics, photographs, and even full-motion video clips, with the possibility of manipulation of the positions of items as well (such as placing pictures in the correct position on a time line, for example).

♦ *Possibility of tutorial format.* Questions missed by a student could be recycled and reappear later in testing, encouraging learning during the test itself, as well as remediation of incorrect responses.

---

* All web site addresses that follow were available at the time of writing of this book in early 2008.

♦ *Self-pacing.* In CAT test takers can work at their own rate. If desired, the speed of responses could also be recorded for additional assessment.

In the following assessment situations, CAT tests are especially beneficial:

♦ Classrooms or programs with exceptionally large enrollments.

♦ Proficiency pretests, for use in placement. CAT tests are often used at the college level to determine in what course level to place a student (for example, Ohio State University's MultiCAT test of French, German and Spanish students.)

♦ Practice tests for any high-stakes test such as the GRE, SAT, or state proficiency examinations.

Figural Response Item Testing

Figural response item testing is a form of assessment used often in science, in which computers are used to administer a graphics-oriented assessment: For example, as a biology assessment, students might be asked to assemble a plant cell from a menu of cell components or transform isomers of molecules using on-screen computer tools. Again, this is a good adaptation for students with learning disabilities, enabling them to still show their comprehension of the basic concepts of the unit. Testing scores on such tests have shown a positive correlation to students' verbal and figural aptitudes, which means they should be a reasonable form of assessment of student performance in science.

There are other examples of this form of assessment in other subject areas as well, such as Tenth Planet's geometry program, which allows students to recognize patterns and manipulate figures and shapes to show their understanding of them, or the Thinking Reader software for students reading below grade level, which helps them learn to summarize, reflect, question, and predict; quizzes in the software test recall, inference, and vocabulary as well as tracking student (and whole-class) performance; it can print six different kinds of reports to monitor improvement.

Other Types of Technology Use

4-Step Planning Must Come First

Before implementing technology practices such as those that follow, I strongly suggest taking the following four steps to avoid frustration and inefficient lessons.

1. Understand your own personal technological proficiency. Practice the technology before asking your students to do so. Evaluate whether the technology is worth the time and effort involved.

2. Determine student needs and technology skills. A brief survey on students' comfort levels and past experience with different formats is important.

3. Determine the technology (and tech support) available. Check availability of the equipment, make sure the software will run on it, and always have a back-up plan ready in case the technology fails.

4. Do a trial run. Try everything at the same time of day students will use it; often a site that functions well at night is overloaded during work hours, or one that works well when just you are on it will run extremely slowly when 20 or more students attempt to access it all at once.

E-Portfolios

E-portfolios are like regular portfolios (see Chapter 5), but are stored electronically. As in any portfolio, students collect their work, select specific pieces for featuring in the portfolio, reflect on what they demonstrate in each piece, set goals (or a direction) for future learning, and celebrate successes by sharing these with a real or virtual audience. An e-portfolio can be formative, with teachers, peers, or online reviewers providing feedback to students, or it can be summative. There are many formats to use in constructing an electronic portfolio:

♦ Simple word processing

♦ Videotape/DVD storage

♦ Web pages

♦ Multimedia software such as HyperCad or Hyperstudio (especially for music or art)

Increasingly, colleges are looking at portfolios for an honest measure of what a student can do; students who develop a portfolio for you will have achieved something really useful for them.

If you need a place to post your e-portfolio online, there are many options available, depending on whether you have your own server or need a hosted solution. I'd suggest consulting Dr. Barrett's "Online Portfolio Adventure," where she discusses as well as compares and contrasts the various options. She updates her site frequently: http://electronicportfolios.org/myportfolio/versions.html/.

Here is a generic rubric for an e-portfolio:

Criteria	Wow	Wonderful	Proficient	Somewhat Proficient	Incomplete	PT
Selection of artifacts	You found really unusual items to include.	**15 points** All samples of work are directly related to the purpose of the e-portfolio.	**11–13 points** Most samples of work are directly related to the purpose of the e-portfolio.	**10 points** Few samples of work are directly related to the purpose of the e-portfolio.	**8 points** Most samples of work are unrelated to the purpose of the e-portfolio.	
Written component		**15 points** All writing demonstrates use of clear, well-organized, and accurate language.	**11–13 points** One or two written samples are unorganized, difficult to interpret, or inaccurate.	**10 points** Three or four written samples are unorganized, difficult to interpret, or inaccurate.	**8 points** Five or more written samples are unorganized, difficult to interpret, or inaccurate.	
Reflection		**15 points** All reflections clearly discuss achievement of goals, critique the work included, and identify goals for continued learning or alternative projects or work.	**11–13 points** Most reflections clearly discuss achievement of goals, critique the work included, and identify goals for continued learning or alternative projects or work.	**10 points** A few reflections discuss achievement of goals, critique the work included, and identify goals for continued learning or alternative projects or work.	**8 points** No reflections discuss achievement of goals, critique the work included, or identify goals for continued learning or alternatives.	

Criteria	Wow	Wonderful	Proficient	Somewhat Proficient	Incomplete	PT
Multimedia use	Creativity and original ideas are obvious in every selection.	**15 points** ♦ Photos, graphics, video, and/or sound are used. All of are of high quality and appropriate. ♦ Information is included concerning the size of all files when providing links.	**13 points** ♦ Photos, graphics, and/or sound are used. Most are edited, of high quality, and appropriate. ♦ Information is included concerning the size of all files when providing links.	**10 points** ♦ Photos, graphics, video, and/or sound are used. A few are of poor quality, or inappropriate. Some aspects overpower the content. ♦ Information is included concerning the size of all files when providing links.	**8 points** ♦ No photos, graphics, video, and/or sound are used, or the ones used are of poor quality, are unedited, or have inconsistent clarity or sound. Selections distract from the content. ♦ Information is included concerning the size of *all* files when providing links.	
Captions	Creativity and original ideas are obvious in every selection	**5 points** Each item has a caption that explains the importance of that particular work, including title, author, and date.	**4 points** Most items have a caption that explains the importance of that particular work, including title, author, and date.	**3 points** Some items have a caption that explains the importance of that particular work, including title, author, and date.	**2 points** None of the items has a caption that explains the importance of that particular work, including title, author, and date.	
Navigation ease		**10 points** All items connect back to the table of contents or home page. All links work correctly.	**8 points** Most items connect back to the table of contents or home page. Most links work correctly.	**6 points** Some items don't connect back to the table of contents or home page. Some links work correctly.	**4 points** There are many problems with links and many sections don't connect to the table of contents or home page.	

Criteria	Wow	Wonderful	Proficient	Somewhat Proficient	Incomplete	PT
Layout	Creativity and original ideas are obvious in every selection	**5 points** All elements ♦ are easy to read (fonts and colors). ♦ use space appropriately, horizontally and vertically. ♦ have a background that enhances the content.	**4 points** Most elements ♦ are generally easy to read (fonts and colors). ♦ use space appropriately, horizontally and vertically. ♦ have a good background. ♦ A few format changes would improve this.	**3 points** Most elements ♦ are often difficult to read (fonts and colors). ♦ use space inappropriately, horizontally and vertically. ♦ have a distracting background. ♦ Some formatting is under- or overused.	**2 points** Most elements ♦ are difficult to read (fonts and colors). ♦ use space inappropriately, appearing cluttered. ♦ have a distracting background. ♦ Most formatting is under- or overused.	
Mechanics		**10 points** There are no errors in grammar, spelling, capitalization, or punctuation.	**8 points** There are few errors in grammar, spelling, capitalization, or punctuation.	**6 points** There are more than 4 errors in grammar, spelling, capitalization, or punctuation.	**4 points** There are more than 6 errors in grammar, spelling, capitalization, or punctuation.	
On time: 10 points					**Total Points: /100**	

♦ Take your students to this web site from Alternative High School for a great tutorial on how to do a portfolio: http://schools.cbe.ab.ca/b863/New%20portfolio%20tutorial/Home.htm/.

For examples of portfolio use, try these web sites:

♦ High Tech High, in California, which is a charter school, has this tutorial for the digital portfolios they require: http://www.hightechhigh.org/dptutorial/index.php/.

♦ At Ligon Middle School, in Raleigh, North Carolina, students created passports to the world, originally with only one online computer: http://www.ncsu.edu/ligon/passports.html/.

♦ Quite a few school web sites have links to this tutorial on creating e-portfolios using Microsoft Word and Excel: http://electronicportfolios.com/portfolios/howto/WordPortfolios.pdf and this one for Adobe Acrobat: http://electronicportfolios.com/portfolios/howto/AcrobatEPortfolios.pdf/.

Of course, there are literally hundreds of commercial e-portfolio software vendors, including many textbook publishers.

WebQuests

A WebQuest is an online inquiry-oriented project format in which most or all the information that learners work with comes from the web. The model was developed by Bernie Dodge at San Diego State University in February, 1995, and the *definitive* web site for information on how, when, and where is found at http://webquest.org/index.php/.

In a WebQuest, students are directed to selected Internet sites to find information to assist them in learning a topic and then making a specified product. Some examples are having them learn about the 1930s and 1940s by making all old sound clips available asking them to produce a radio play complete with sound effects, learning about Lewis and Clark while giving students the task of creating a board game about them, reading conflicting viewpoints about cloning, or participating in a discussion about what government policies should be on this subject.

A WebQuest is scaffolded into steps (good for slower learners) and encourages higher-level thinking. It is a really good project to assign (to either complete a WebQuest, or to write one), especially for compacting or spin-offs. My favorite site to do this is TrackStar, where there are many already written and ready to use or modify: http://trackstar.4teachers.org/; but there are other places to do this as well, such as Filamentality http://www.kn.att.com/wired/fil/ (which isn't as user friendly, and they *clean out* sites every so often so that with no warning your Quest may be gone; but it does really have a good step-by-step tutorial when you write your first WebQuest).

To see some more examples of WebQuests created by teachers for differentiated classrooms, in many subjects and assorted according to topic and grade level, go to http://www.rockwood.k12.mo.us/itech/webquests/wqmatrix/matrix.htm/.

Blogs and Chats

A blog (short for *web log*) is similar to a personal web page, with one major difference: A web page is mostly about displaying or disseminating information, and a blog is more interactive. A web page just sits there, but a blog evolves as the student and others exchange information. It is another project option for students to investigate, a way to show what they can do, online, as well as elicit feedback and further information from readers.

A blog has the following:

♦ A topic of interest (which can change over time): Initially, the blogger (person who originates the blog) posts his or her own thoughts and waits for comments or information from others who visit the blog.

♦ A way to receive comments and make those visible to future visitors.

♦ A format: The most common is to show postings in chronological order, but some might have links for postings on more than one topic, or links to related web sites. Other features might include music, video, photos, podcasts, and even archives.

♦ A site: Make sure yours is not blocked by your school server, such as many currently popular blogs like myspace.com!

In any subject that features communication as an important element, blogs can be invaluable and easily monitored by the teacher. In addition, currently it is easy to find a free blog-creation site. I have had students use http://www.blogger.com successfully. Google now offers a free one as well.

How could a blog be an assessment? I have used it most often as an option for compacting: The student selects a topic and sends out invitations to post comments. Then, he or she prints out the blog and writes (or orally reports, or makes a poster/collage), a reflection piece on what information the blog yielded on the topic. My students have also been able to post a certain number of comments in a *virtual community* called Viv@ (http://www.ardecol.ac-grenoble.fr/viva/school/index.htm) as part of a tic-tac-toe assignment or a homework grid, or as part of their Flex Plan. A virtual community is just a blog with a visual component to separate the topics found there.

A *chat room* is an online conversation that happens in *real time*, as everyone participating is on the site, typing messages at the same time. Messages that are typed in by a user appear instantly to everybody in that chat room. Chat rooms are a preferred method of communication for students and are also effective communication channels for the disabled, confined, and distance learning situations; it is also a terrific formative assessment, because it allows students to practice concepts while discussing them.

In a situation where communication is desirable, such as a debate or discussion of a topic (current events class, English, science issues such as global warming or stem cell research, and so on) can be done online just as easily as aloud; and other schools (from other countries, even; I've done chats with France) or groups can be invited to join. When the chat is over, you can print out the chat to give feedback and/or evaluate the number and quality of postings.

The drawbacks to chat rooms are that most places where one could be established are open to anyone who might Google it, and some of those people might post inappropriate language or topics. You might look for one where you could serve as moderator (postings go to you first, to read and approve, before they appear to others). You should also want to make the chat room as private as possible.

Telementoring

Telementoring (also known as e-mentoring, cyber-mentoring, computer mediated communication [CMC], or virtual mentoring) is the electronic version of mentoring. Traditionally, a mentor is a person with more knowledge, expertise, and skills who shares this with a (generally younger) person (often called, humorously, the *Yoda factor*). In this case, the sharing is done via e-mail, blogs, or other online applications such as audio or video conferences or instant messaging, independently of time or place. The electronic aspect enables people to interact who otherwise might never meet, across time zones and even continents or hemispheres. Most telementoring is either for educational or career-related purposes. I am currently a telementor for three in-service teachers and, often, for a group of student teachers. It is both interesting and rewarding.

There are three basic types of mentoring: pair mentoring, group mentoring, and *ask an expert* mentoring, which all seem self-explanatory. The main difficulty seems to be locating the right expert, who is willing to be a mentor. Mentors can come from local universities or community colleges, online, in the business sector, and among parents of young people.

Uses for telementors:

◆ Proofreaders for compositions

◆ Tutors in various subject areas

- Resources for information for research papers in many subject areas

- Models and advisors for career interests

- Encouraging student use and familiarity with various computer skills such as proofreading, spell-checking, sending messages, videos, photos, and so forth

- Pen pals to encourage interest in writing skills

Free telementoring projects include the following:

- *Business*: Hewlett Packard's International Telementor Program, since 1995, has used e-mails between HP employees and students at www.telementor.org/.

  - WITI (Women in Technology) http://www.witi.com/ has mentorships for young women who want to move into the business world.

  - For blind or visually impaired students interested in a career in business, there is MentorMatch at http://www.careerconnect.org/cnib/home.asp/.

- *All subjects*: http://www.mentoring.org/ 25 of the 50 states have mentor programs set up on this site for a variety of activities, with examples and testimonials.

  - *Personal learning coaching* is the British term for mentor, at http://www.personallearningcoaching.com/.

  - Electronic Emissary sets up mentors for almost any topic at http://emissary.wm.edu/.

  - Students can join global projects at http://www.kidlink.org/KIDPROJ/KIDPROJ is like a *family* who talk to each other, participate in many discussions, and work together on many different activities and projects.

  - More kids collaborating on projects to change the world are at http://www.iearn.org/.

  - A hotlist for contacting museum curators, organized by the types of museums, is at http://sln.fi.edu/tfi/hotlists/museums.html/.

  - AskAnExpert tries to find answers to questions on almost anything at http://www.askanexpert.com/.

- *Language arts*: The Read*Write*Now project at http://www.tnellen.com/cybereng/mentor/partners.txt/.

- *Mathematics*: Ask Dr. Math at http://mathforum.org/dr.math/.

- *Science*: The Ask an Expert link at Scientific American is at http://www.sciam.com/askexpert_directory.cfm/.

  - Journey North engages students in a global study of wildlife migration and seasonal change. Students in K–12 share their own field observations with classmates across North America at http://www.learner.org/jnorth/index.html/.

  - Globe is a hands-on program that will link Oceanic and Atmospheric students with other students and with scientists around the world. Students, guided by trained teachers, take environmental measurements identified and designed by an international group of scientists and educators at http://www.globe.gov/.

  - MadSci Network has a page where students can post science questions at http://www.madsci.org/.

  - George Lucas' web site Edutopia has quite a few projects students can do or join, and is great for ideas, at: http://www.edutopia.org/projectbasedlearning.

  - TestBed has quite a few collaborative projects going at teaparty.terc.edu/about/about.html/.

- *Social studies and science*: Global SchoolNet Foundation (GSN) brings together youth online from 194 countries to explore community, cultural, and scientific issues that prepare them for the workforce and help them become responsible and literate global citizens at http://www.globalschoolnet.org/index.html/. You can design your own project or join an existing project created by other teachers and students.

- *History*: National History Day sponsors challenging contests for students at http://www.nationalhistoryday.org/.

  - The National Writing Board reviews papers at http://www.tcr.org/nwb/index.htm/.

- *Psychology*: The Social Psychology network mentors anyone interested in becoming a psychologist: http://www.socialpsychology.org/mentor.htm/.

- *Visual arts*: ACME professional animators acts as mentors for high school students at http://www.acmeanimation.org/.

- *Practical arts*: Ace Mentor serves high school students of engineering, construction and architecture at http://www.acementor.org/.

♦ *Music:* Just Plain Folks gives advice to anyone interested in being in the music industry at http://www.jpfolks.com/Mentors/index.html/.

Finally, in addition to seeking a telementor, encourage students to keep a journal where they write down their expectations, things they have learned and thoughts about the final outcome, and share their mentoring experiences with their peers.

Online Publishing

Web publication has quite a few advantages over traditional types of publication.

Online publishing

♦ Is faster and less expensive than traditional publication.

♦ Provides a real, immediate, authentic audience that can even give feedback to writers; and let them know their work is valued. This sense of audience is highly motivating.

♦ Gives purpose to the process of writing.

♦ Lets students control the format and content of their works (and even revise, modify, and update it) as well as target a specific audience if desired.

♦ Lets anyone do it, not just those selected by juries or editors.

♦ Works not just for writing, but for other creative endeavors, including music and art.

♦ Is limited only by the web-authoring skills of students and teachers.

♦ Can be quickly and easily viewed.

Advanced placement classes often use this format for research papers, as you will quickly find if you use a search engine. Here is a quick list of sites where students can publish for free, in alphabetical order.

♦ *The Concord Review*: http://www.tcr.org/

♦ *Crunch* from NCES is currently being redesigned, but here's what the site says right now:

Are you a budding poet? A movie or game critic? A world traveler? Then Crunch needs you! We're gathering articles, poems, reviews, and artwork for the next issue of Crunch. E-mail us your artwork and writing for consideration: kidszone@ed.gov/. The web site is at http://nces.ed.gov/NCESKids/CRUNCH/

♦ *Global Children's Art Gallery*: http://www.naturalchild.com/gallery/

- *Global Wave* the Young Writers Club (TWYC) online magazine: http://www.cs.bilkent.edu.tr/~david/derya/gw/

- *KidProj*: http://www.kidlink.org/KIDPROJ/projects.html allows postings in a variety of languages

- *KidsCom: http://www.kidscom.com/create/write/write.html*

- *Kids Space*: http://www.kids-space.org/index.html has sites for artwork, musical compositions, stories, and more

- *KidzPage* publishes poems: http://www.veeceet.com

- Submit articles about your hero at *My Hero*: http://www.myhero.com/home.asp

- *The National Student Research Center*: http://youth.net/nsrc/nsrc-info.html publishes student research in science, math, social studies, consumerism, language arts, and multidisciplinary

- *Scholastic* has a long list of sites that not only teach various types of writing (including scientific) but provide a place to publish them for feedback: http://teacher.scholastic.com/activities/index-learn.htm#index

- *Science Class Challenge* from CAPC, which are new each year: http://nocfcs.org/scc/home.htm

- *Storybook Online*: http://www.storybookonline.net/Default.aspx

- *Storyteller*: http://www.edbydesign.com/storyteller/index.html

- At *Tess Pet-Sitters Club* students continue a story that's already begun: http://www.abbyandtess.com/story.html

- *Writer's Window*: http://english.unitecnology.ac.nz/writers/home.html

Students work much harder to perfect a product that will actually be published; online publishing is a great motivator!

Summary

The graphic below should help you see how the various technological forms of assessment discussed in this chapter would fit into your assessment needs, according to the desired differentiated method and whether it is best suited for use as a formative or summative evaluation.

Differentiation by	FORMATIVE	SUMMATIVE
Content	WebQuest Telementoring	
Process	E-portfolio Chat Telementoring	E-portfolio
Product	Blog E-portfolio	Blog CAT Online publishing WebQuest

7

How to Implement Differentiation

Baby Steps

First and foremost, do *not* try to do everything in this book at once. Please just pick one type of formative assessment (because research shows that formative assessment shows the largest effect on scores, including those of standardized tests) and keep trying, adapting it until you think you are comfortably using it. Then, and only then, try another one.

Also, remember to use variety, not the same thing over and over. Assess in a variety of ways and over a period of time, not just once at the end of the unit (remember, formative is the most effective). This might require an attitude change. Assessment is often associated with feelings of being confused or overwhelmed, insecurity, guilt, frustration, or anger: It is deeply social and personal for the student as well as the teacher creating and administering the assessment. Taking baby steps should help everyone avoid those feelings.

Third, learn from your colleagues. Chances are you are partially interested in differentiation because your administrators want you to use it. (If you're just doing it because you know it's better for the students, bravo!) Is anyone else in your school using differentiation? Teachers need to see living examples of implementation, done by teachers who inspire them and to whom they can go for support as well. However, even with the examples of others, there are a lot of little practical details you'll need to work out for yourself, especially how you'll be grading (I'll give you some suggestions in this chapter).

Try to get extra support for the additional planning time and time to reflect on what happens as you implement differentiated assessment, to have some training or to train others, and to collect evidence of the effectiveness of what you've tried. Two-thirds of the staff at my school met voluntarily once a week to ask questions and share plans, successes, and failures. When our principal learned of this, he was able to find a grant that could pay us for this time.

Finally, be patient. Remember, learning new skills takes time. Everyone has to find his or her own differentiation strategies that mesh well with the familiar patterns of classroom work.

Well, enough generalities. Let's talk about some common issues.

What to Do With Early Finishers

Most teachers in differentiated classrooms have anchor activities that students can go to after completing a test. These same activities are appropriate for students who finish the work on a unit early, are compacting, are waiting to hear from a telementor, need a change of activity, and so forth. These most often include:

- ♦ journal,
- ♦ book report,
- ♦ portfolio,
- ♦ research project,
- ♦ activity packet, and
- ♦ WebQuest,

but could also be things like a KWL for the next unit, a crossword or word Sudoku, a *brain buster* to solve, interest centers (manipulatives, kits, puzzles, realia, etc.), vocabulary work, accelerated reader or silent reading assignment, magazine articles with general questions or activities, listening stations, or even some tutoring of a classmate who was absent and needs to be caught up. The sorts of work advocated for compacting (Chapter 5) would also be good anchor activities.

The key is to have something *meaningful* (not busy work!) and *tied to classroom content and instruction* (and if it's exciting to do, or at least interesting, so much the better). It should also not be something that takes you away from assisting students still working on the unit assignment.

They also need to be activities whose behaviors and expectations have been previously taught, and ones that students will be held accountable for in terms of on-task behavior and task completion.

Managing Grades

At workshops on differentiation, I often hear mutters of "too much work" and "I grade things only once!" As I said, differentiation involves adjusting how you do things; and in this section I'd like to share some strategies and advice, both my own and gleaned from others. But first, here are the most important and basic things to do:

- ♦ *Make practice (homework) assignments pass/fail.* Give credit for it being done, if you must; but expect students to make mistakes, and don't penalize them when they do.

- ♦ *Give students multiple attempts to master something, with no penalty for having to try again.* I highlight errors, and then require corrections to be made (easy: the second time, just look at the highlighted portion). Requiring corrections helps students note the types of errors they make and continues the learning process (or begins it, if they copied their work from someone else). This means I generally have two grades, rough draft and final, for every assignment.

- ♦ *Assess in the same ways that material was learned and practiced.* If they learned it via listening, the assessment should include listening. Many experts even say not to rearrange the classroom and that tests should not be given by substitute teachers for this same reason; your presence (stance, tone of voice, etc.) may trigger memory for some types of learners. Haven't you ever noticed students looking toward where you had had a poster or visual aid for material on the test?

- ♦ *Make sure students understand what will be assessed, and how.* There shouldn't be any *gotcha* questions or surprises for students.

- ♦ *Grades should reflect what students can do, know, learned, or mastered.* Nonacademic factors like attendance and behavior should not figure into the grade if you are measuring skills. According to McTighe (in Wiggins & McTighe, 1998), if you truly wish to differentiate, give grades for progress (growth), achievement (excellence) and effort (task completion).

Some authorities, such as Rick Wormeli, are *very* against giving group grades, as well (2006).

If you can avoid the preceding things, you can expect results like these:

I saw kids who had failed until seventh grade being willing to take a risk and try on some assignments. Instead of a grade, I wrote feedback to let kids know what improvements were needed and what they were doing right. As the year went on, I got more class work and homework turned in than I ever did when it was part of the grade. I saw kids become more confident in their abilities, and grades reflected what the kids could do. I was amazed at the difference! —Lisa Pierce, secondary teacher (Wormeli, 2006, p. 115)

Tracking Task Completion

Now, let's talk about what you should do instead of avoid. Let's begin with the easiest one (but the one you might have been wondering most about): task completion, called "progress" by McTighe (Wiggins & McTighe, 1998). This means keeping track of all assignments and whether they have been done. For homework, I have a simple system: All grades are worth the same number of points, and I award half the points for the first draft and the other half when a final, corrected copy is turned in. Other, more creative teachers have a graphics approach to this type of assessment. Remember the tic-tac-toe–style Vocab Grid in Chapter 3? That could be used as an assessment: Take a stamp and for each one they complete, award up to 20 points based on completion and accuracy (students will have used a checklist or rubric available to them on the wall or in a folder, so there should be no surprises) for a total of up to 100 points after the completion of five assignments. It is easy to see, at a glance, whether everything has been completed.

Another easy-to-use assignment is a *Homework Calendar*. There is even a very accessible web site for creating and/or posting a calendar (if your school web site doesn't have one) at http://assignaday.4teachers.org/. Students who are absent are still expected to have work in on the day it is due, or the first day they return. A colleague who uses one also uses a stamp, saying, "When students arrive they are to place their homework calendar and homework on their desk and do their warm-up. If the homework is not out, I do not stamp it. It's rough in September, but then it gets easier."

If students are doing projects, make sure you break those down into steps such as topic handed in and approved, detailed plan, list of sources, rough draft, peer evaluation, and so on; and dedicate a spot in the grade book for each step. If the class is differentiating for product, it is quite likely that students will reach these steps at different times; a glance at the grade book (or a checklist on the wall, if that is legal where you teach) tells both you and the students who is making progress and who needs to proceed faster.

The second easiest is excellence: This is the final grade for the project, or the chapter or unit assessment score.

The grade you'll probably need to think about is the one for growth. This should take two forms:

1. Self-assessment by the student

2. Assessment by the teacher

Both forms of assessment should use the same rubric, one that is given to students the first week of classes. Using a *growth* grade really helps lower-level students put forth more effort, as well as improving their grade. Recently, there was a case in the *New York Times* of a student who needed a class to graduate, and took it three times, improving her score each time but not enough to pass the final. Incorporating a growth or effort element in her grade might have made the difference for her between passing and failing.

Controversy Over Grade Recording Methods

Everyone, other than new teachers, has usually evolved his or her own method of grading that is comfortable and workable; so in this section I'm merely going to report on various methods used by differentiating teachers, in hopes one is a variation of something you already do, or something you think might be a comfortable fit with how you intend to differentiate. Grading practices vary widely between subject areas, as might the limitations of the system your school uses for recording grades. None of these are better than the others, and in fact, I list the pros and cons of each as I go through them.

Grouping by Standard, Objective, or Benchmark

This method might be best for you, especially to show parents and/or administrators that these are foremost in your mind in designing your classroom instruction. Ken O'Connor supports this kind of reporting: to "not set up grading plans according to methods of assessment" (2002, p. 50–51) but to assess learning goals.

For example, in a science class, the three objectives might be analysis, synthesis, and prediction. So, for the analysis section, you would record grades for a test, an essay, question answers, and any report. For the synthesis portion, you might record any vocabulary quizzes, a test on the periodic table, a comic strip about covalent vs. ionic bonds, or other creative endeavors. And for the prediction section, you might include a test on predicting alkalinity, an activity on the behavior of inert gases, and lab reports that require prediction of results before their performance.

Pros: This method shows progress in achieving objectives well.

Cons: You might need to use a weighted grades system, because some objectives have many more assignments than others. Also, some objectives might stretch beyond the grading period, and you'd need a plan on how much of that objective needs to be covered for each grading period.

Grouping by Weight or Category

This method is just like it sounds: tests in one section, homework in another, and so on.

Pros: This method quickly shows exactly how many of each a student has done, plus point totals for each.

Cons: You might need a separate grade book page for each, unless you know exactly how many of these to expect through in a grading period (not a problem with most electronic grade books, though). Also, if you differentiate by tiering, some students' test grades or points-per-unit might have a different total possible than others, unless you carefully structure the assignments for each tier to have the same number of points, weights and categories.

Recording Grades Chronologically

If recording grades chronologically, I suggest color coding them, because different kids proceed at different chronological rates. For example, if you write in the test scores using a green pen, you could look quickly to see who is missing a green entry or quick-count the green entries to see if all tests have been taken.

Pros: Chronological entry would also assure that students have done something every day as blank spaces would be easy to spot.

Cons: Some projects might take many days to do, and in that case you would need students to keep an activity log (see Chapter 5) and assign some sort of points for keeping it.

Monitoring Student Progress: Behavioral Problems and Solutions

The acronym PRAISE is, in a nutshell, the best way to plan behavior management: Being *p*roactive, using *r*einforcements, *a*ssessing and analyzing the *i*ntent of misbehavior, being *s*incere, and *e*mpowering students are the keys to a positive and structured classroom environment. Praise and encouragement in PRAISE are essential elements of a differentiated classroom:

Proactive teachers appropriately arrange the classroom; post rules as well as classroom rewards and consequences; clearly define expectations; and create a positive, structured environment (Wong & Wong, 1998). Where does differentiation figure in? Planning challenging lessons is also a form of being proactive. Many students act out because lessons are either too difficult or too boring. Differentiation requires giving challenging and interesting assignments, as well as giving choices. Giving a variety of choices is also being proactive. Students who can choose what to do are happier in the classroom.

Reinforcements need to be built into any classroom behavior, and these can be negative or positive reinforcement. Experienced teachers use a pat on the back, eye contact, or physical proximity. These first two parts seem very basic but they are crucial and can handle most situations.

Assessing misbehavior such as chronic disruptions or disrespect for others involves observing and collecting information on who, what, and when: what happens before it occurs, what is the behavior, and what happens following the behavior.

Intent: Students generally misbehave for one of the following reasons: attention, power, revenge, or inadequacy. There are books written on how to deal with these; and because this isn't really caused by differentiation, I'll refer you to more expert opinions than my own for this. My own (inexpert) advice would be to build a relationship based on trust and honesty and try to find areas of common interest.

Sincerity involves showing students that you want what is best for them: You want them to succeed. In helping them to self-evaluate, and by making your expectations clear and fair as to what will be assessed and how, you should easily achieve this aspect.

Empowerment is an essential element of both behavior management and of differentiated assessment. The first step is that the teacher must allow students to give opinions and suggestions. A differentiated classroom is not totalitarian. Students must be able to choose projects and topics of study, to work individually or together, and so forth. They also need to learn to set goals and even establish the criteria and rubrics for classroom activities.

When assigning an activity, ask students to describe what a good-quality example of that activity might be. Their opinion should then become what they are evaluated on. Their list of specifics could become a checklist for an *A* product. As they list them aloud, write them down, and have them write their own copy. I have observed significant improvement in work handed in after taking the time in the beginning to have students list the characteristics of a good poster, PowerPoint, speech, crossword puzzle, or whatever it may be. You can make suggestions as well (such as, "Does everything need to be spelled correctly?"); but as they do the assignment, they are motivated to please their classmates and not just their teacher. They are also crystal clear on the expectations, because they provided them. It is easy for them to self-evaluate their work, and there are few surprises as to what grade it will receive, because they originated the criteria. One side effect of this is that you won't experience many parent complaints, because students perceive your classroom as caring and fair to them. In addition, students feel their opinions are important in assessment, and they have a sense of shared ownership over, and pride in, their learning.

Next Steps

I like to advocate some *action research* in the classroom. As you read this book, what strategies appealed to you? Did any sound almost like something you do, or like something a colleague does, and who might be a good partner for you as you attempt the same thing?

1. Choose a form of summative assessment you'd like to try (Chapters 4, 5, and 6).

2. *Preassess* yourself: Choose a unit you think would be a good *fit* for differentiation, possibly one with which you were less than satisfied in the past. List the skills and ideas students must master for that unit. Correlate those to your curriculum and standards.

3. *Preassess* students (Chapter 2) to determine whether to differentiate content, process, or product.

4. Begin differentiated instruction.

5. Use frequent *formative* assessments (see Chapter 3); and, if possible, chart student growth (or have them self-evaluate) on the content standards and skills for the unit. To formatively assess yourself as a differentiated teacher, remember to carefully monitor your students (body language, frustration level, etc.) and adjust instruction as needed.

6. Involve students in setting the evaluation criteria for the summative assessment.

7. Use your chosen *summative assessment* from step 1.

8. Compare student scores to the last time you taught the unit.

9. Ask students for feedback on the unit.

10. Use the data gathered in steps 8 and 9 to review the unit as taught, and plan for next time you teach it. Evaluate the effectiveness of differentiation, and don't forget to figure in your own comfort/ease (e.g., methods for keeping track of student work, ease of assessment, access to support, and so on).

11. Report on what you have learned to students, parents, colleagues, or administrators. Celebrate successes (growth in learning, curriculum mastery, etc.).

12. Keep trying this form of summative assessment until you feel comfortable with it. Then try another, and another.

Appendix 1

Useful Lists

Skills to Assess

Analyzing

Articulating thoughts

Asking questions

Brainstorming

Building skills

Classifying

Combining/integrating

Communicating with others

Comparison/contrast

Comprehending

Creative problem solving

Detecting bias

Developing a point of view

Developing a strategy

Developing ideas

Developing insights

Developing vocabulary

Elaborating

Evaluating

Expanding interests

Finding data

Finding problems

Finding solutions

Fluency

Identifying connections

Imagining

Justifying content

Logical sequencing

Making analogies

Making inferences

Organizing ideas/content

Paraphrasing

Persevering

Predicting

Recalling

Recognizing patterns

Seeing relationships

Self-awareness

Self-motivation

Self-reflecting

Sequencing

Summarizing

Synthesizing

Transferring

Verifying inferences

Visualization

Wondering

Ways to Show What You Know

A

action plan
adventure
advertisement
advice column
album
anagram
analogy
analysis

anecdote
anecdote
animation
annotated bibliography
annotated reading list
anthology
apparatus
application

aquarium
archaeological excavation
art show
artifact collection
audiotape recording
autobiography
award

B

ballad
ballet
banner
belief statement
bingo game
biographical presentation
bio-poem

block picture story
blueprints
book
book jacket
booklet
bookmark
book report

brainteaser
brochure
bullet chart
bulletin board
bumper sticker
business letter

C

calendar
campaign speech
caption
card game
cartoon
CD cover
celebrity profile
ceramic
characterization
charades
chart
checklist
children's book
choral reading
cinquain
classification key

classified advertisement
classroom decoration
classroom design
Claymation video
closed ecosystem
clothing
collage
collection
comedy act
comic book
commentary
commercial
community service advertisement
comparison
comparison chart

computer graphic
computer model
computer program
computer simulation
concept map with words missing
construction
contest
conversation
cookbook
costume
couplet
coupon
creative writing
critique
crossword puzzle

D

dance
database
debate
definition
demonstration
description
design a structure
design a new product

design a new animal
diagram
dialogue
diary
dictionary entry
dictionary game
diorama
directions

directory
discussion
display
dissection
documentary
document-based question
dramatization
drawing

E

editorial
editorial cartoon
equipment
essay

etching
evaluation
exaggeration

exhibit
explanation
eyewitness account

F

fabric
fairy tale
field trip
film
finger puppet(s)
first aid/first aid kit
fish pond

flag
flannel board
flash cards
flip book
flip chart
flow chart
follow-the-clues game

food
food chain/web
forensic lab
free verse
friendly letter
furniture

G

gadget
gallery
gallery walk (guided)
game
garden
genetics family to show inheritance pattern

globe
glossary
gossip column
graffiti wall
grant request
graph

graphic organizer
greeting card
guidebook
guided tour
guidelines

H

haiku
hand puppet
handbook
handout
hat

headline
hieroglyphic
history
hypercard card stack of material for test
hypercard clip art file

hypercard review questions
hypothesis
hypothetical diary
hypothetical journal

I

illustrated glossary
illustrated story
illustration
imprint
instruction manual

instrument
interdisciplinary presentation
interior monologue
interview (written or filmed)

invention
investigation
invitation

J, K

Jeopardy game
jigsaw puzzle
jingle
job description

job shadowing
joke
journal
kite

L

lab experiment
lab research project
landscaping plan
law
learning center
learning safari
lecture

lesson plan
letter
letter of complaint
letter of opinion
letter of request
letter of support
letter to editor

limerick
list
log
logo for shirt
lyrics

M

machine
macramé
MAD (Make a Difference) project
magazine article
manual
map
marionette
mask
meeting
memorandum
mentor

metaphor
mime
mind map
mnemonic
mobile
mock trial
model
monologue
montage
monument
mosaic
movement

movie
multimedia presentation
mural
museum
museum walk
music
music video
musical
mystery
myth

N

narration
nature museum
nature trail
needlework

newscast
newsletter
newspaper
newspaper advertisement

newspaper article
new story ending
notes
nursery rhyme

O

oath
obituary
observation
observation log
Olympics

one-minute lesson series
one-minute reading
opinion poll, analyzed
oral report

order
order form
origami
outline

P

painting
pamphlet
panel discussion
parable
parody
pattern
pedigree
peer assessment
pen pal letter
performance
petition
photo essay
photograph
Pictionary game
picture dictionary

pin
plan (house, travel)
plan a balanced menu or diet
plan a computer search
plan a field trip
plan a hypothetical trip
plan a nature walk
plan a recycling program
planet description
play
playing cards
poem
political cartoon
pop-up book

portfolio
postage stamp
post card
poster
prediction
press conference
progress report
prophecy
protest an injustice
public relations campaign
public service announcement
puppet show
puzzle

Q

quatrain
question

questionnaire
quilt

quiz

R

radio announcement
radio commercial
radio show
rap
rebus story
recipe
recommendation
reenactment/recreation
reflection

reply
report
report using only graphics
reproduction
request
research investigation
research report
resume
review

revision
rewrite
rhyme
riddle
risks and benefits chart
robotics organism
role-play
room
rubric

S

scale drawing
scale model
scavenger hunt
scoring guide
scenario
schedule
science fiction story
scrapbook
script
scroll
sculpture
selection
self-assessment
seminar
series of letters
series of posters

share knowledge with family/friend
shopping list
short story
show-and-tell
sign
silk screen
simulation
skit
slideshow
slogan
soap opera
soil test
solar-powered item
solution
solve a community problem

song
sound effects
speech
stencil
stick puppet
story
storyboard
story problem
storytelling
study cards
study journal
subject dictionary
summary of notes
survey
symbol

T

take-home exam
talk show
tall tale
teach a class
telegram
television newscast
terrarium

test
theory (formulate and defend)
ticket out (exit ticket)
time capsule
timeline
tools
town map

toy
training session
translation
transparency
travel advertisement
travel log
tutor someone

U, V

utopia (describe)
Venn diagram
verdict

videotape
videotape review
visual aid

vocabulary list

W

wall hanging
wanted poster
warm-up
warrant for arrest
weather map

web
web page
WebQuest
woodcut
word game

word search
work sample
writing

X, Y, Z yearbook prediction

zodiac chart

zoo map

Assessments Classified
By Gardner's Intelligences

Verbal/Linguistic
Say it
Write it

advertisement	fairy tale	poster
anecdote	family tree	prediction
book report	interview	radio broadcast
brochure	jokes	recipe
bulletin board	journal	recitation
code	lesson	reflection paper
comic strip	letter	report
commercial	menu	role play
comparison	monologue	script
creative writing	news article	simulation
crossword	newscast	skit
debate	oral report	slogan/jingle
demonstration	outline	Socratic seminar
description	pamphlet	song
dialogue	panel discussion	speech
diary	parody	story
diorama	petition	telephone message
discussion	plan	weather forecast
essay	play	
explanation	poem	

Visual/Spatial
Picture it

album	charades	flag
animation	chart	flipbook
art gallery	clothing	flowchart
art project	collage	game
award	costume	graph
banner	cover	hat
board game	demonstration	hidden picture
book jacket	diorama	illustration
bookmark	display	labeled diagram
bulletin	drawing	map
bumper	etching	mask
cartoon	film	maze

mobile	political	slideshow
model	pop-up book	sticker
mosaic	portrait	story cube
movie	postage stamp	storyboard
mural	postcard	tee-shirt
painting	poster	television program
papier-mache	PowerPoint	theater set
photo essay	prototype	transparency
photos	scroll	video
picture book	sculpture	web site
play rebus story	sketch	

Logical/ Mathematical
Count it

advertisement	experiment	model
annotated bibliogra-phy	fact	outline
	family	petition
brainteaser	file	play
bulleted list	flowchart	puzzle
chart	game	recipe
checklist	graph	riddle
code	hidden picture	survey
collection	labeled diagram	timeline
comparison	lesson	transparency
crossword puzzle	map with legend	travel log
database	maze	tree
debate	menu	Venn diagram
demonstration	mobile	
edibles		

Bodily/Kinesthetic
Move it

art project	experiment	painting
ballet	film	parody/spoof
calligraphy	flipbook	play
card game	food	play performance
charades	gadget	press conference
clothing	game	puppets
costumes	graph	puzzle
dance	learning center	readers theater
demonstration	machine/invention	skit
diorama gadget	mime	television program
display	model	video
dramatization	musical instrument	
etching	needlework	

Musical/Rhythmic
Hum it

album	dance	performance
audio recording	film	play an instrument
ballad/rap/song	improvisation	poem/rhyme
choral reading	jingle	riddle
compilation/tape	lyrics	video
concert	music	

Interpersonal
Lead it

advice	fairy tale	petition
animation	film	plan a campaign
build a consensus	game	plan an event
bulletin board	interview	play
chart	journal	press conference
choral reading	lesson	role playing
comic strip	maze	survey class opinions and present results
debate	mentor	
demonstration	museum	television program
discussion	pamphlet	volunteer project
editorial essay	paraphrase	write a new law
exhibit	peer assessment	

Intrapersonal Reflect on it	advice	comic strip	journal
	belief statement	diary	learning center
	book report	editorial essay	poem
	bulletin board	fairy tale	self-evaluation
	chart	family tree	time line
	collection	goal setting	

Naturalistic Investigate it	bulletin board	guess/hypothesis	solution to a problem
	classification	journal of observations	song
	collection	photoessay	time line
	description	scientific drawing	
	display	scrapbook	

Performance Prompts From Bloom's Revised Taxonomy

Use this list as a reference to see at what level you are asking your students to perform and to help with grids, projects, tiered assessments, and many more.

Remembering

◆ Remember previously learned info

arrange	label	recognize
choose	list	rehearse
combine	match	relate
compile	memorize	repeat
copy	observe	review
count	outline	select
dance	name	show
define	play (sport, instrument)	sing
describe		sketch
draw	point	spell
fill in	quote	state
find	rap	tell
hunt	recall	write on board
identify	recite	

Understanding

◆ Demonstrate meaning of info

act	extend	recognize
categorize	find more about	report
chart	generalize	research
classify	give examples	restate
compare	identify	retell
conclude	infer	review
correct	interpret	reword
demonstrate	locate	rewrite
describe	outline	show
differentiate	paraphrase	summarize
discover	predict	translate
discuss	put into your own words	visualize
explain		

Applying

♦ Apply info to a real situation

adapt use	draw a map	practice
apply	experiment	prepare
build	incorporate	produce
calculate	interpret	record
change	interview	reformat
choose	listen	reread
command	manipulate	research
construct	mime	revise
convert	model	role play
demonstrate	modify	sequence
diagram	operate	share
discover	order	simulate
display	organize	solve
dramatize	plan	translate

Analyzing

♦ Break info into parts/see how they relate

analyze	debate	organize
appraise	deduce	reflect
brainstorm	dissect	research
categorize	distinguish	select
choose	examine	separate
classify	experiment	simplify
compare	infer	solve
conclude	inspect	survey
connect	interpret	test for
contrast	investigate	
critique	question	

Creating
♦ Rearrange info into something new

award	disprove	plan
build	dispute	produce
cartoon	explore	propose
caricature	generalize	rearrange
combine	hypothesize	refine
compose	improvise	reorganize
conclude	infer	report
construct	influence	revise
create	invent	rewrite
design	make	satirize
determine	measure	transform
devise	organize	write
develop	originate	
discuss	perform	

Evaluating
♦ Make judgments about info

adapt	decide	persuade
appraise	defend	predict
argue	discriminate	prioritize
assess	elaborate	prove
build	estimate	rank
change	evaluate	rate
choose	feel	recommend
combine	forecast	select
compile	grade	self-evaluate
consider	imagine	support
convince	improve	suppose
craft	judge	theorize
criticize	justify	value
critique	modify	verify

Appendix 2

Differentiated Assessment Terms

♦ **Adjusted questioning**

Adjusted questioning is when a teacher alters the word choice and complexity of discourse or text to accommodate students' prior knowledge and current level of knowledge. This is a simple way to differentiate for individual students or small groups within the same class, and is especially used with ELL students, those whose native language isn't English.

♦ **Anchor activity**

An *anchor activity* is a meaningful content-related activity that students can do independently, allowing small groups to meet with the teacher for conferencing on formative results, project check-ups, and other parts of differentiated assessment. Common examples are reading a book of choice, writing in a journal, filling in a graphic organizer, and so forth.

♦ **Authentic assessment**

Because I don't believe students should ever be asked to perform work that is not authentic in nature, I treat these terms (authentic assessment, alternative assessment, or performance assessment) synonymously. This form of assessment can be defined as any procedure that asks a student to create or construct an answer (perform) and/or requires students to show what they know and can do in a meaningful, real-world application (authentic). It is considered *alternative* because it does not involve a traditional pencil-and-paper test. Some other characteristics are that students know in advance what the criteria for their performance are and often have input in deciding what those will be. These assessments are scored on a point scale based on well-defined criteria (a rubric) that is also presented in advance. Performance assessment requires students to be active participants who are learning even while they are being assessed (see Chapter 4).

♦ Bloom's taxonomy

Bloom's taxonomy is commonly known as a hierarchy important to any classroom instruction, whether using differentiation or not; but it can be an important guide to whomever is wishing to implement differentiation of assessment. In it, six levels of learning are established:

1. *Remember/recall* basic facts, vocabulary, or lists of things like countries and capitals, plot and characters in a story.

2. *Understand* concepts underlying basic facts, and so forth, such as categories they belong to, how they work, and so forth.

3. *Apply* information learned to a written or oral task. Examples are to write a letter, or perform appropriately in a simulation (speaking or listening).

4. *Analyze* the structure or parts and their purpose.

5. *Evaluate* material and make a judgment about it based on self-selected (or teacher directed) criteria or other factors.

6. *Create* something new using learned material, with an emphasis on creativity.

Teachers often talk about *Bloom verbs*, especially when writing tiered assignment plans. There's a good list of these in Appendix 1.

♦ Choice chart

In a *choice chart*, the teacher gives students who have completed a required activity a list of choices of activities. These may be arranged by types of activities (oral, written, listening), by subject (grammar, vocabulary, culture), by skill level (easy, more challenging), by time frames, or by learning styles or multiple intelligences.

♦ Compacting

Compacting involves examining curriculum to eliminate concepts, principles, or skills that have already been mastered. A teacher gives a pretest, or uses a survey or KWL, to determine students' true instructional levels. After determining which students already have a good understanding of a given concept, the teacher then gives those students choices of (usually independent) activities for their class time while the others are brought up to speed by the teacher. In my opinion, this is best used for short periods of time. This method helps to avoid boredom for more advanced students, and gives the teacher fewer students on which to concentrate for remedial instruction (see Chapter 5).

◆ Design-a-Day

This interest-based strategy lets students decide what to work on for a class period (or several). They specify goals, set time lines, and assess their progress. This is a good early step in preparing students for longer projects in similar format.

◆ Formative assessment

Formative assessment is frequent, continuous assessment during a period of study for checking on student progress, giving feedback, and making decisions to shorten, modify, or otherwise adjust the course of study (see Chapter 3).

◆ Graphic organizer

A *graphic organizer* is any kind of design, drawing, outline, web, or diagram that assists students to arrange information visually is a graphic organizer. Commonly used examples are Venn diagrams, flow charts, semantic maps, or KWL charts (see Chapter 1).

◆ KWL chart (sometimes KWLU)

A *KWL chart* (sometimes *KWLU*) stands for *K*now, *W*ant to know, and *L*earned (or *K*now, *W*ant to know, *L*earned, and *U*se), the captions for a three- or four-column chart or graphic organizer.

K	W	L	U

This is a great strategy to use when compacting: Have students write what they already know about a topic (reminding them of prior knowledge—great in upper levels when beginning a unit that expands on a previous year's learning) in the first (K) column. Then have them write what they want/wish to know (W) in the next column. As they write, the teacher can look at their work and see what they remember and what sorts of interests in this topic the class has. This method also mimics aspects of the inquiry process and is a perfect fit with what an effective reader should do. As they proceed during the unit, the third column (L) is used to record what is learned. A fourth column (U) is sometimes used as an assessment piece for students to show what they've learned or to list real life applications for the knowledge gained.

◆ Learning contract

As the name suggests, this is a *negotiated*, written agreement between student and teacher about what tasks will be done by the student, when the due dates for these tasks are, and the criteria for evaluation. This is used for several forms of differentiated instruction, especially compacting (see Chapter 5).

◆ Learning style

There are many different classifications of *learning styles*, which can be defined as the best method for a given student to process, remember, and use information. Gardner has eight (see *multiple intelligence theory*) and others classify students on a brain-based module: left-brained or right-brained; 4MAT uses personality characteristics. A teacher aware of students' learning styles can plan lessons and activities that are more beneficial to students. See Appendix 1 for lists of projects assorted according to Gardner's intelligences as well as Bloom's taxonomy.

◆ Metacognition

Metacognition is a psychological term for the process of learning how you learn things best (learning style).

◆ Multiple intelligence theory

Multiple intelligence theory: Howard Gardner states that there are 8 different intelligences, or learning styles.

1. Verbal/linguistic
2. Musical-rhythmic
3. Logical-mathematical
4. Interpersonal
5. Intrapersonal
6. Bodily-kinesthetic
7. Visual-spatial
8. Naturalistic

Knowledge of these styles and activities to appeal to them, as well as which of these are represented in the classroom, is essential to differentiated instruction. (Strategies are listed in Appendix 1.)

◆ Portfolio

A *portfolio* is an assessment that involves collection samples of student work along with charts and documents that show clearly that the works selected for the portfolio are evidence of setting goals, striving to achieve them, and reflection on the process and results of the process of preparing the portfolio. These can be creative and are an excellent way of organizing student input for a differentiated classroom (see Chapters 5 and 6).

◆ Preassessment

Done before beginning the instructional portion of a unit, *preassessment* shows the teacher (and the student) what is and is not known about a topic. This is essential before setting goals for the unit, or dividing into study groups. There are many forms of preassessment (see Chapter 2).

◆ Scaffolding

Scaffolding gives structure to learning and is essential for students who need things broken down into small steps. Graphic organizers, cloze sheets, dialogues, short-answer worksheets, and even crosswords (but only ones that might involve processing information such as putting on verb endings, solving problems, reading a time line) may be scaffolding methods. The goal of scaffolding is for students to someday not need scaffolding but to build autonomy (see Chapter 1).

◆ Summative assessment

Completed at the end of a unit of study, it requires students to demonstrate mastery of all essential understandings; a grade is generally assigned (see Chapters 4, 5, and 6).

◆ Tiered assignment

Usually organized in three difference levels, *tiered assignments* are a method of giving students a choice in the depth and complexity of a task for a given unit. The teacher can assign particular students to a level based on a preassessment or allow students to choose. Of course, the summative assessment for a tiered unit should also reflect the level at which the student asked (or was asked) to perform.

◆ WebQuest

A *WebQuest* is a teacher-designed lesson that uses the Internet to allow students, individually or in groups, to move through a process of researching, drawing conclusions, and developing a presentation about a specific topic. These can be differentiated for student readiness but are easiest to use as an interest-based differentiation strategy (see Chapter 6).

Appendix 3
Checklists

Board Game

Student _____ Classmate _____

☐ ☐ Name for the game
☐ ☐ Game uses material learned in class
☐ ☐ At least 20 questions
☐ ☐ Questions are clear and accurate
☐ ☐ Rules are clearly explained: easy to play
☐ ☐ At least 4 people can play it
☐ ☐ Board is attractively decorated, with appropriate graphics
☐ ☐ Game was interesting/fun to play

Brochure

Student _____ Classmate _____

☐ ☐ Illustrations mixed with text where appropriate
☐ ☐ Included material not already learned in class
☐ ☐ Well organized (no repetitions)
☐ ☐ Information is up to date
☐ ☐ Information is correct
☐ ☐ Well-balanced layout on page
☐ ☐ Correct spelling
☐ ☐ Correct grammar
☐ ☐ Student's name is on project

Cartoon

Student _____ Classmate _____

☐ ☐   Illustrations neatly drawn
☐ ☐   Writing is easy to read
☐ ☐   Correct spelling
☐ ☐   Correct grammar
☐ ☐   Conveys a message
☐ ☐   Humorous
☐ ☐   Colorful
☐ ☐   Student's name is on project

Chart

Student _____ Classmate _____

☐ ☐   Well-organized sections
☐ ☐   Has a title and subtitles
☐ ☐   Writing is clear and neatly done
☐ ☐   Spelling is correct
☐ ☐   Information is correct

Collage

Student _____ Classmate _____

☐ ☐   Colorful
☐ ☐   Title/labels spelled correctly
☐ ☐   Easy to understand theme/message
☐ ☐   Solid backing
☐ ☐   Creative and original
☐ ☐   Pictures overlap
☐ ☐   Only a narrow margin without pictures
☐ ☐   Student's name is on project

Comic Book/Comic Strip

Student _____ Classmate _____

☐ ☐ Colorful
☐ ☐ Easy to read
☐ ☐ Uses pictures and words to tell the story
☐ ☐ Accurate spelling
☐ ☐ Frames in correct sequence
☐ ☐ Characters clearly drawn
☐ ☐ Humor
☐ ☐ Dialogue
☐ ☐ Original/creative
☐ ☐ Student's name is on project

Concept Map

Student _____ Classmate _____

☐ ☐ Main idea in center
☐ ☐ Easy to read
☐ ☐ Shows details about the topic
☐ ☐ Shows relationships of details to one another
☐ ☐ Information on topic is correct

Crossword Puzzle

Student _____ Classmate _____

☐ ☐ Correct spelling
☐ ☐ Words intersect each other in at least one space
☐ ☐ Indicates clues for Across and Down
☐ ☐ Numbered
☐ ☐ Clues are accurate definitions of the words
☐ ☐ Neatly and clearly done
☐ ☐ Answer key provided

Diorama

Student _____ Classmate _____

- ☐ ☐ Realistic depiction of scene
- ☐ ☐ Sides have background scenery
- ☐ ☐ 3-dimensional objects in foreground
- ☐ ☐ Accurate
- ☐ ☐ Has a label/title
- ☐ ☐ Durable construction
- ☐ ☐ Student's name is on project

Flipbook

Student _____ Classmate _____

- ☐ ☐ Required size
- ☐ ☐ Five different categories
- ☐ ☐ At least two details for each category
- ☐ ☐ Easy to use
- ☐ ☐ Correct spelling
- ☐ ☐ Correct grammar
- ☐ ☐ Student's name is on project

Flowchart

Student _____ Classmate _____

- ☐ ☐ Items in correct sequence
- ☐ ☐ Easy to read
- ☐ ☐ Shows relationship between items by using arrows or other types of lines
- ☐ ☐ Short explanation of each item
- ☐ ☐ Accurate information
- ☐ ☐ Correct spelling
- ☐ ☐ Neatly written
- ☐ ☐ Student's name is on project

Listening Activity

3 points for each question/response. Responses may be written or oral (no matching!).

- ☐ Didn't require more than one repetition
- ☐ Complete response
- ☐ No errors in response

Note: Another item I sometimes put in: 1 point for a *basic* response, and 2 points for an *elaborated* response. Example: If the prompt is "What sports do you play?" an elaborated response would be not just the sport, but where, when, and with whom they play it, or that they won a game, and so forth.

Mobile

Student _____ Classmate _____

☐	☐	Colorful
☐	☐	Included material not already learned in class
☐	☐	Easy to read
☐	☐	Easy to understand why elements were chosen
☐	☐	Accurate information
☐	☐	Correct spelling
☐	☐	Student's name is on project

Oral Presentation

10 points

Student _____ Classmate _____

☐	☐	Understood question/prompt
☐	☐	Spoke more than basic requirements (supporting examples and details)
☐	☐	Spoke with ease/flow and enthusiasm
☐	☐	Used a variety of sentence structure and vocabulary
☐	☐	Spoke at an appropriate volume level
☐	☐	Evidence of preparation
☐	☐	Eye contact
☐	☐	Correct pronunciation
☐	☐	Correct grammar
☐	☐	Spoke for an appropriate length of time

Poster

Student _____ Classmate _____

☐ ☐ Color used
☐ ☐ Large picture or illustration
☐ ☐ *All* writing large enough to read from across the room.
☐ ☐ Neat (not messy)
☐ ☐ Organized
☐ ☐ All important information found on poster
☐ ☐ Accurate information
☐ ☐ Correct spelling
☐ ☐ Correct grammar
☐ ☐ Creativity of presentation
☐ ☐ Interesting to look at/read
☐ ☐ Student's name on project

PowerPoint

Student _____ Classmate _____

☐ ☐ Information is up to date
☐ ☐ Information is interesting
☐ ☐ Included material not already learned in class
☐ ☐ Picture is appropriate
☐ ☐ Sound is appropriate (sound is optional)
☐ ☐ Effects (optional) used enhance, not distract
☐ ☐ Pacing: not too slow, not too fast
☐ ☐ Well organized
☐ ☐ Font color contrasts sharply from background
☐ ☐ Font size is easy to read across room
☐ ☐ Font style is easy to read
☐ ☐ Correct spelling
☐ ☐ Correct grammar
☐ ☐ Student's name is on project

Storyboard

Student _____ Classmate _____

☐	☐	Setting is clear
☐	☐	Characters have names and personalities
☐	☐	Conflict (man vs. man, nature, self) exists
☐	☐	Several actions take place
☐	☐	Uses several words of vocabulary from the unit
☐	☐	Uses several elements from the original story
☐	☐	Uses color
☐	☐	Writing is neat and legible
☐	☐	Correct spelling
☐	☐	Correct grammar

Storybook

Student _____ Classmate _____

☐	☐	Setting is clear
☐	☐	Characters have names and personalities
☐	☐	Conflict (man vs. man, nature, self) exists
☐	☐	Several actions take place
☐	☐	Uses several words of vocabulary from the unit
☐	☐	Has a moral/meaning/theme that is obvious
☐	☐	Uses color
☐	☐	Writing is neat and legible
☐	☐	Correct spelling
☐	☐	Correct grammar

Tee Shirt

Student _____ Classmate _____

- ☐ ☐ Uses color
- ☐ ☐ Uses information from research/reading
- ☐ ☐ Meaning is easily understood
- ☐ ☐ Appropriate for school wear
- ☐ ☐ Correct spelling
- ☐ ☐ Correct grammar
- ☐ ☐ Oral presentation of product to class

Video

Student _____ Classmate _____

- ☐ ☐ Interesting beginning
- ☐ ☐ Sound quality good
- ☐ ☐ Dress and props appropriate
- ☐ ☐ Pace: not too slow, not too fast
- ☐ ☐ Seriousness of performers
- ☐ ☐ Accurate information
- ☐ ☐ Correct pronunciation
- ☐ ☐ Correct grammar
- ☐ ☐ Interesting ending
- ☐ ☐ Student's name is on project

Written

20 points

Student _____ Classmate _____

☐	☐	On task in class
☐	☐	Objectives met
☐	☐	Correct format for paper (font, etc.)
☐	☐	Neat
☐	☐	Ideas clearly expressed
☐	☐	Easily understood by intended audience
☐	☐	Careful choice of words
☐	☐	Content shows knowledge of subject
☐	☐	Specific details are used related to topic
☐	☐	Details are accurate/correct
☐	☐	Organized presentation
☐	☐	Variety of sentence structures
☐	☐	Variety of vocabulary used
☐	☐	Illustrations (if appropriate)
☐	☐	Characterization good (if appropriate)
☐	☐	Evidence of editing
☐	☐	Title reflects subject
☐	☐	Correct spelling
☐	☐	Correct grammar
☐	☐	Student's name is on project

For anything else, there is a really good online checklist generator at http://pblchecklist.4teachers.org/checklist.shtml/.

Bibliography

Beauchamp, L., McConaghy, G., Parsons, J., & Sanford, K. (1996). *Teaching from the outside in.* Edmonton, Alberta, Canada: Duval House Publishing, p. 45.

Black, P., & William, D. (1998). *Inside the black box: Raising standards through classroom assessment.* Retrieved January 22, 2008, from http://www.pdkintl. org/kappan/kbla9810.htm

Blaz, D. (2006). *Differentiated instruction: A guide for foreign language teachers.* Larchmont, NY: Eye on Education.

Curry School of Education, University of Virginia. (2006). *Frequently asked questions,* Retrieved January 28, 2006, from http://curry.edschool.virginia.edu/ hottlinx/tier1/faq/faq.htm

Dochy, F., Segers, M., & Buehl, M. M. (1999). The relations between assessment practices and outcomes of studies: The case of research on prior knowledge. *Review of Educational Research, 69*(2), 145–186.

Dreikurs, R., Grunwald, B. B., & Pepper, F. C. (1998). *Maintaining sanity in the classroom: Classroom management techniques* (2nd ed.). Philadelphia: Taylor & Francis.

Farago Cramer, S. (Fall 1994). Assessing effectiveness in the collaborative classroom. *New Directions for Teaching and Learning,* n59, pp. 69–81.

Flint, Nerilee. *Educational assessment: students' perceptions of fairness.* Paper presented at the Australian Association for Research in Education Conference, November 29 to December 3, 1998. Abstract retrieved January 22, 2008, from http://www.aare.edu.au/98pap/fli98304.htm

Gresham, Oregon School District. (1992, draft). *Portfolio guidelines in primary math.* Multnomah, Oregon.

Heacox, D. (2001). *Differentiating instruction in the regular classroom: How to reach and teach all learners, grades 3–12.* Minneapolis, MN: Free Spirit Publishing.

Marzano, R.J., Pickering, D.J., & Pollock, E. J. (2001). *Classroom instruction that works: Research-based strategies for increasing student achievement.* Alexandria, VA: Association for Supervision and Curriculum

Miner, W. S., & Finn, A. (2003). Middle school teachers' preassessment practices and curricular/instructional modifications. *Research in Middle Level Education Online, 26*(2). Retrieved January 22, 2008, from http://www.nmsa. org/ Publications/RMLEOnline/tabid/101/Default.aspx

National Science Foundation. (2002). Evaluation and types of evaluation. In *The 2002 user-friendly handbook for project evaluation.* Retrieved January 22, 2008, from the National Science Foundation at http://www.nsf.gov/pubs/2002/nsf02057/nsf02057_2.pdf

O'Connor, K. (2002). *How to grade for learning: Linking grades to standards* (2nd ed.). Thousand Oaks, CA: Corwin Press.

Reis, S. M., Westberg, K. L., & Kulikowich, J., et al. (1993). *Why not let high ability students start school in January? The curriculum compacting study* (Research Monograph No. 93104). Storrs, CT: The National Research Center on the Gifted and Talented, University of Connecticut.

Riel, M. (2000). A title IX for the technology divide? In D. T. Gordon (Ed.), *The digital classroom* (pp. 161–167). Cambridge, MA: The Harvard Education Letter.

Rodabaugh, R. C. (1996). Institutional commitment to fairness in college teaching. In L. Fisch (Ed.), *Ethical dimensions of college and university teaching* (pp. 37–45). San Francisco: Jossey-Bass.

Stiggins, R. J., Arter, J., Chappuis, J. & Chappuis, S. (2004). Chapter 11. In *Classroom assessment for student learning: Doing it right—Using it well* (pp. 335–360). Portland, OR: Assessment Training Institute. Good discussion of student self-assessment.

Strickland, C.A., & Tomlinson, C. (2005). *Differentiation in practice: A resource guide for differentiating curriculum grades 9–12*. Alexandria, VA: Association for Supervision and Curriculum Development.

Taylor, C. S. & Nolen, S. B. (2005). Chapter 10. In *Classroom assessment: Supporting teaching and learning in real classroom* (pp. 123–147). Upper Saddle River, NJ: Pearson-Merrill-Prentice Hall.

Tomlinson, C. (1995). *How to differentiate instruction in mixed-ability classrooms*. Alexandria, VA: Association for Supervision and Curriculum Development.

Whitley, B., Jr., Perkins, D., Balogh, D., Keith-Spiegel, P. & Wittig, A. (July/August 2000). Fairness in the classroom. *APS Observer, 136*. Retrieved January 22, 2008, from http://www.psychologicalscience.org/teaching/tips/ tips_0700.cfm

Wiggins, G. (1997). *Show what you know as you go*. Retrieved January 22, 2008, from http://www.edutopia.org/node/291

Wiggins, G., & McTighe, J. (1998). *Understanding by design* (p. 68). Alexandria, VA: Association for Supervision & Curriculum Development (ASCD).

Willis, E. M., & Raines, F. (2001). Technology in secondary teacher education: Integration, implications and ethics for the changing roles of teachers. *T.H.E. Journal, 29*(2), 54. Retrieved January 22, 2008, from www.thejournal.com/articles/ 15589

Wong, H. K., & Wong, R. T. (1998). *The first days of school: How to be an effective teacher*. Mountain View, CA: Harry K. Wong Publications.

Wormeli, R. (2006). *Fair isn't always equal: Assessing & grading in the differentiated classroom*. Portland, ME: Stenhouse Publishers.

Printed and bound by PG in the USA